Translations from Greek and Roman Authors

SOPHOCLES

Electra · *Antigone* · *Philoctetes*

Sophocles

Electra · Antigone · Philoctetes

TRANSLATED BY KENNETH McLEISH

PUBLISHED BY THE PRESS SYNDICATE OF THE UNIVERSITY OF CAMBRIDGE
The Pitt Building, Trumpington Street, Cambridge, United Kingdom

CAMBRIDGE UNIVERSITY PRESS
The Edinburgh Building, Cambridge CB2 2RU, UK http://www.cup.cam.ac.uk
40 West 20th Street, New York, NY 1001–4211, USA. http://www.cup.org
10 Stamford Road, Oakleigh, Melbourne 3166, Australia
Ruiz de Alarcón 13, 28014 Madrid, Spain

First published 1979
Sixth printing 2000

Printed in Great Britain by
Athenæum Press Ltd, Gateshead, Tyne & Wear

ISBN 0 521 22010 6 paperback

Library of Congress cataloguing in publication data

Sophocles.
Electra: Antigone; Philoctetes.
(Translation from Greek and Roman authors)
Bibliography: p.
I. McLeish, Kenneth. II. Sophocles. Antigone.
English. 1978. III. Sophocles. Philoctetes. English.
1978. IV. Title. V. Series.
PA4414.A2M3 1978 888′.01 78-51679
ISBN 0 521 22010 6

Contents

Translator's note

There is no consistency in the transliteration of Greek names. The governing factor has in every case been ease of reading. For the same reason, long lines of Greek have occasionally been divided into groups of shorter lines in English, and a number of 'paragraph-breaks' inserted in the longer speeches. Line-numbers throughout refer to this text, not the Greek.

A brief bibliography is given on page 160.

I am greatly indebted to my friends Guy Lee and William Shepherd for help and encouragement during the preparation of this book.

Electra

The legend

Agamemnon, King of Argos, angered the goddess Artemis by killing one of her sacred deer. Later, when he was preparing to lead the Greek fleet against Troy, she took her revenge. She held back the winds, and refused to let the fleet sail until Agamemnon sacrificed his own daughter Iphigenia for fair weather.

Ten years later, when Agamemnon came home victorious from the Trojan War, his wife Clytemnestra avenged Iphigenia's death. She and her lover Aegisthus hacked Agamemnon to pieces with an axe (in Sophocles' version of the story, while he sat at the dinner table). Aegisthus married Clytemnestra, and became king in Agamemnon's place.

Orestes, the young son of Agamemnon and Clytemnestra (who should have succeeded to his father's throne), was sent away to safety in Phocis, in case his mother and step-father butchered him as well. The two daughters of Agamemnon, Electra and Chrysothemis, stayed in Argos, in the royal palace of Mycenae, waiting for the day when Orestes, grown up, would return and punish his father's murderers.

The play

Sophocles' play begins at the end of this time of waiting. He is not concerned to tell us what happened next, as a modern playwright might be. (The Greek audience knew the rest of the legend: how Orestes killed his mother and her lover, and eventually ended the chain of blood and revenge that had haunted the royal family for so long.) Instead, he is particularly interested in showing us the characters of the three women, Electra, Clytemnestra and Chrysothemis, and their relationship with each other.

The three parts give magnificent opportunities to actors – in the Greek theatre to male actors, not female. Chrysothemis is a young girl, trying hard to do what is right, against all difficulties. Clytemnestra is a character like Shakespeare's Lady Macbeth (also written for a male actor): a queen sure of her authority, prepared to go to any lengths to keep up her power. (The scene where she prays to Apollo, with the seemingly immediate answer of the god, the arrival of the false messenger, is one of the most striking in the play.) The part of Electra calls for skill in speaking (and sometimes singing) dramatic poetry: her laments with the Chorus and her long, fiery speeches require an actor of unusual ability.

Electra is written in particularly formal, patterned verse. The Chorus parts are often organised in pairs of paragraphs, each with the same rhythm and sequence of ideas. The dialogue scenes (usually between only two characters at once) begin with long balancing speeches, and quicken into sections where the characters speak alternating lines, each the same length as the one before, and with thought balancing thought, argument balancing argument (see for example pages 36 and 41).

Sophocles is well known for this balance and control, and for the purity and simplicity of his poetry. One of the most striking things about *Electra* is the way he uses such balanced, controlled means to express violent and complex emotions. The formal style adds tension to the drama, and allows him to highlight his characters' feelings and motives as well as the simple events of the story itself.

The first production of *Electra* was in about 415 B.C.

Electra

CHARACTERS

ORESTES	ELECTRA
PYLADES	CHRYSOTHEMIS
SERVANT OF ORESTES, an old man	CLYTEMNESTRA
	AEGISTHUS

SLAVES

CHORUS OF THE WOMEN OF ARGOS

An open courtyard outside the palace of Mycenae in Argos. In the background, the palace doors; to one side, a small altar.
Dawn.
An old man, Orestes' SERVANT, *comes in from the side, followed by* ORESTES *and* PYLADES. *They are dressed in travelling clothes.*

SERVANT
Orestes, son of Agamemnon, son
Of the warlord who led the Greeks at Troy,
We are in Argos – the ancient land
You pined for, and longed to see again.
Look, over there: the sacred plain
Of Io, child of the river-god;
Down there, the Lycean Agora, named
For Lycean Apollo; there, on our left,
The famous temple of Hera. This place,
Where we are standing now, is Mycenae –
Golden Mycenae, rich in death,
Palace of the dynasty of Pelops.
When they butchered your father, I took you
Away from here, on the orders of Electra
Your sister. I saved you, I brought you up
To manhood, to avenge your father's death.

Orestes, and Pylades dearest of friends,
We must make our plans at once.

The dark blanket of stars is put away,
And birds are carolling the rising sun.
Before anyone stirs, it is time to talk.
Our long waiting is over: now we must act.

ORESTES

My faithful friend, everything you do,
Every word you say, proclaims your loyalty.
Just as a thoroughbred shows its mettle
Even in old age, pricking up its ears
And snorting at danger, so you are first
With good advice, first with encouragement.
This is my plan. Listen carefully,
And if I miss the target, guide my aim.

I went to consult Apollo's oracle,
To ask the god how I was to avenge
My father and punish his murderers.
This was the answer:
'Go yourself, helped by no army.
Use tricks to snatch the punishment.
They killed; they must die.'

The god's oracle was clear; we must obey.
When the moment comes, you must find a way
To get inside the palace and spy on them.
Bring back a clear report. No one inside
Will recognise you after all these years.
An old man with white hair – who will suspect?
Tell them this story. You are a visitor
From Phocis, sent by the lord Phanoteus,
Their most trusted ally. You bring news –
And this you must confirm with a solemn oath –
That Orestes is dead, in an accident
At the Pythian Games:
In the chariot-race, he was thrown and killed.
Make that your story. While you are telling it,
The two of us will visit my father's grave,
As Apollo commanded. We shall make
Tomb-offerings: wine, and a cut lock of hair.
Then we'll come back, bringing the bronze urn
You know of, hidden in the wood – and trick
Our enemies with the glad news they long for,
That my body is burnt to ash, and gone.

A bad omen, to call the living dead?
By pretending death I live again;
I avenge my father, and win fame.
Deeds, not words – there's nothing to fear.
There are stories of wise men of old
Who pretended death and came to life again,
Reborn to glory greater than before.
So I shall be born from pretended death,
A new, bright star to scorch my enemies.

O Argos my country, O gods of home,
Welcome me! Smile on my journey!
O palace of Agamemnon my father,
I have come, with the gods, to end this plague –
Don't drive me away! My own kingdom –
Let me restore it, and win the throne!
God grant my prayers. And now, to work, old man.
You know your orders: see they are obeyed.
We'll go, and play our part. For all of us
The moment of fate is now: we must use it well.

ELECTRA (*inside*)
O Zeus! O Zeus!

SERVANT
Orestes, listen! Someone's crying . . .
There, inside. Some unhappy slave-girl.

ORESTES
Or else my sister, unhappy Electra.
Shall we stay here a moment, and listen?

SERVANT
No: we must put Apollo's orders first.
Hurry to Agamemnon's grave, and make
The offerings. That is the surest way
To win success, and bring us victory.

They go.
After a moment a small door is opened in the large palace doors, and ELECTRA *comes out. She is dressed in poor, slave's clothes.*
As she speaks, the Chorus of WOMEN OF ARGOS *comes in, singly, and in small groups. They speak, sometimes separately, sometimes together. Some of their words would have been accompanied by music and choral movement.*

ELECTRA

Light of the morning,
Sky-canopy above,
As the shadows of night
Melt into day, hear me:
I am desperate with grief,
I tear my own flesh raw.
In this palace of pain
My bed tells a tale of tears
For my father dead.
He did not die nobly in battle,
Feasting with Ares in a foreign land:
My mother, and Aegisthus
Her bedmate, like foresters,
Split his skull with a blood-red axe.

I am the only one to mourn
Your death, Agamemnon, father,
Your sharp, cruel death.
To the shimmering stars,
To the light of day,
I shall weep unending tears.
Like the nightingale who killed her child
I shall cry out my grief
Here at my father's gate
For the world to hear.

O spirits of Hell,
Powers of the Underworld,
Furies, daughters of the gods,
Look at the husband killed,
The marriage-bed defiled.
Punish them! Avenge his death!
Help me; bring Orestes home.
I am crushed with grief,
A burden of pain
Too great to bear alone.

WOMEN

Electra, child, child of the murderess,
Why pine your life away?
Why this gnawing, endless grief
For him, for Agamemnon?

He was caught in the godless snare
Your witch-mother set for him;
He was cheated in death by a criminal's hand.
I say this: they killed, they must die.

ELECTRA

Kind friends,
You have come to comfort me.
I know, I understand.
But you must let me weep,
Let me mourn my poor father's death.
Oh my dear friends,
I beg you,
Let me weep for him,
Oh, let me weep.

WOMEN

He has gone to the shores of Hell,
The resting-place all men must come to.
No tears or prayers will bring him back.
You are eating your life away
In a grief past bearing.
There is no help in tears:
The crime is done, and cannot be cured.
Is it not time to give up this misery?

ELECTRA

Feeble
A child who will not grieve
For her father dead.
I am like the nightingale,
God's messenger, crying 'Itys! Itys',
Forever sorrowing. I am like
Niobe, all tears,
A goddess of stone
Weeping, weeping.[1]

WOMEN

Electra, my child, you are not alone
In your tears, alone of all mankind.
You share the grief that racks you so
With your own sisters, here in the house:
Chrysothemis, and Iphianassa too.
And there is another,
Fretting out his youth in hiding,

Waiting for the happy day
When Zeus will guide him
Home to royal Mycenae:
Orestes, the exile, returned at last.

ELECTRA

Orestes! Does he know how I wait for him?
I have no husband, no children;
Day after day, uncomforted,
I bear my burden, weep useless tears.
Does he know of the crimes committed,
The wrongs I tell him? Does he care?
He says he is longing to be here –
Why does he say so, and never come?

WOMEN

Electra my child, do not despair.
Lord Zeus is still master in heaven:
He sees, and knows, and rules all things.
Your anger racks you: leave it to him.
You can blunt your fury's edge
And still not forget your father.
Time is a soothing, healing power.
Your brother, Agamemnon's son,
In his seaside home by the pastures of Crisa,
Will not forget; and the lord of Hell,
Avenger of the dead, will remember too.

ELECTRA

The bright flower of my life is withered;
My hope is gone, my strength destroyed.
I have no children to comfort me,
No loving husband to stand by me.
I am no better than a slave,
A drudge in my father's halls.
Dressed in these rags
I stand with the other slaves
And feed on the scraps our masters leave.

WOMEN

There were bitter cries as he came home
From Troy; bitter cries as he took his place
At the table for the feast,
Where a swift sharp axe was waiting.
The witch-wife planned, the lover struck:

Dark powers mingled with men
And the deed was done –
Foul mating spawned a fouller crime.

ELECTRA

Bitter that day
More than all other days;
Bitter that night,
That feast unspeakable.
He saw his own death
Glinting in their hands;
Their fingers gripped me,
Twisted and broke my life.
O Zeus, lord of Olympus,
Punish them with pain,
Deal dreadful death,
Turn triumph to dust.

WOMEN

You have said enough, Electra.
Can you not see that what you do,
What you say, will bring you more pain,
Worse suffering still?
You are sullen and stubborn,
Breeding endless arguments,
A treasury of grief.
If you fight with power, you'll lose.

ELECTRA

I have no choice.
I am on the rack.
My stubbornness is born of pain.
Till my dying breath
I shall feed on this hate.
What words can comfort me?
O my dear friends,
There are no words.
Leave me, leave me:
I am sick, past cure,
Walking a long road
Of endless misery.

FIRST WOMAN

Electra, listen to me.
Trust me. I speak

As a mother to her child.
Do not make bad worse.

ELECTRA

Is there an end to unhappiness?
How is it right to forget the dead?
It's unheard-of: I won't do it.
Even if I lived a life of ease,
Content, I should never clip
The wings of mourning for my father.
If dead men are dust
And nothingness, no more;
If murderers live
Free of the price of blood,
How can we say
That respect and shame
Still exist in the world of men?

FIRST WOMAN

My child, whether you follow our advice
Or not, you'll always find us loyal friends.
Your good is our good, now and forever.

ELECTRA

Dear friends, you must forgive me if I seem
Forever complaining, weeping endless tears.
My life compels it. What else can I do?
What woman of birth, of spirit, would suffer
As I have suffered, and say nothing?
My father, dead. Injustice, flowering
Unchecked. Day and night, an agony of grief.
My own mother, who gave me birth,
Hated, hated. My father's palace, shared
With his murderers. The King! The Queen!
I'm theirs: they allow me life, or death.

Think what it means to see, day after day,
Aegisthus sitting on my father's throne,
Wearing my father's robes. Day after day
I watch him pouring libations to the gods
There at the hearth where he butchered him.
And hardest of all to bear, night after night
I see them together in my father's bed:
The murderer and her – shall I call her

My unhappy mother, or Aegisthus' whore? –
That shameless one, who sleeps with a criminal,
Fearing no Fury;[2] she laughs at what she did,
And makes the day a festival – the day
She tricked my father and murdered him,
The day she celebrates each month with hymns
And offerings to the 'gods who saved the state'.
All this I must watch – here in the palace –
Weeping in misery, mourning alone
At the feast named for my father's death.
When I weep, I weep in secret – this is
No grief to be indulged in public tears.
Even so, the woman they call Her Majesty
Comes up to me and scolds me, saying,
'Cursed of the gods! Are you the only one
To lose a father, the only one on earth
Ever to mourn? Damn you! May the gods
Of the Underworld give you good cause to weep!'

These insults are enough – except when she hears
Rumours that Orestes is coming home.
Then she is wild with fury, stands over me
And screams, 'It's you I have to thank for this!
You did it! You snatched him from my hands
And stole him to safety. You rescued him,
And soon enough you'll pay the penalty!'
So the bitch-mother yaps; and by her side
Her noble bridegroom stands and nods –
Aegisthus, the toothless lion, plague of our state,
The woman-at-arms she nerves to fight.

One day, Orestes will come home and end it.
The waiting has wasted my life with grief.
'He's coming soon,' they said once.
And still they say he's coming. My hope is dead.
O my dear friends, you see how I suffer.
Tell me, why should I hold back my tears?
Why should I show honour or respect?
In a dark world my path is darkness too.

FIRST WOMAN

Where is Aegisthus? These are wild words.
Is he here in Argos or away from home?

ELECTRA
He's away, on his country estates.
If he was here I would have stayed indoors.

FIRST WOMAN
In that case . . . if he's away . . . then perhaps
This is the time to ask . . . if you can say . . .

ELECTRA
He's away. Ask what you want to know.

FIRST WOMAN
Orestes your brother . . . can you tell us,
Is he on his way? Is he coming home?

ELECTRA
We have his promise. We have nothing more.

FIRST WOMAN
A fearful task. All men would hesitate.

ELECTRA
I did not hesitate to save his life.

FIRST WOMAN
The prince will come and save the ones he loves.

ELECTRA
I trust him, or I'd not have lived so long.

FIRST WOMAN
Say no more now. Look: your sister Chrysothemis,
Your dear sister, is coming from the palace.
She brings funeral-gifts,
Tomb-offerings to pay the dead below.

CHRYSOTHEMIS *comes in from the palace.*

CHRYSOTHEMIS
Electra, indoors is the place for women.
You know that. Why do you come out here,
Where all Argos is listening? Will you never learn?
What good does all your empty anger do?
I feel what has happened, too –
I feel it bitterly. If only I dared,
If only I had the strength, I'd show my hate.
But I prefer to bend before the storm;
I'll never threaten what I cannot do.
If this is cowardice, you be a coward too!
I know that you are right and I am wrong –
But I must be free, I can never be a slave:
And to be free, I must bow to the king and queen.

CHRYSOTHEMIS
Listen: this is what I overheard.
You must stop these complaints, or else
They'll have you taken away from here
And walled up forever in a living grave.
You'll never see daylight again;
You'll cry your cries, and no one will hear.
Electra, listen to me! Give way now!
Or else, when the blow has fallen, don't blame me.

ELECTRA
Is that what they plan to do to me?

CHRYSOTHEMIS
When Aegisthus comes home, exactly that.

ELECTRA
If that's all, may the gods send him quickly home.

CHRYSOTHEMIS
What do you mean? What kind of prayer is that?

ELECTRA
A prayer to the gods to send Aegisthus home.

CHRYSOTHEMIS
Are you such a fool? The sooner he comes –

ELECTRA
The sooner he comes, the sooner I'll escape.

CHRYSOTHEMIS
Are you so eager to give up your life?

ELECTRA
My life? A fine life, a life to wonder at!

CHRYSOTHEMIS
It would be if you chose to make it so.

ELECTRA
You mean if I betrayed the ones I love.

CHRYSOTHEMIS
All I mean is this. Bow to the king and queen.

ELECTRA
You bow! You grovel! That's not my way.

CHRYSOTHEMIS
You're mad, and your madness will destroy you.

ELECTRA
Destroy me or not, I shall avenge him first.

CHRYSOTHEMIS
He'll not blame me. He understands, I know.

ELECTRA

It's hard to believe. You are Chrysothemis,
Agamemnon's daughter – and still you place
Your mother first. The advice you offer me
Is hers, not yours. She told you the words to use.
You will have to choose, Chrysothemis:
Will you defy her – like a fool, like me –
Or obey her, and betray the ones you love?
You say if you dared, if you had the strength,
You'd show how much you hate them. Well, then:
I am working to avenge our father –
Will you refuse to help? Will you discourage me?
Must we add cowardice to suffering?

You advise me to accept, to give up my grief.
What good would that do? I have my life:
A life of misery, but I chose it
And I am satisfied. I give them pain,
A grave-gift to make my father smile,
If the dead below can smile. You hate them,
Or so you tell me. But your hate is words,
Not deeds. In all you do, you honour them.

You say I must bow to the king and queen.
Will they reward me with the gifts you love –
Groaning tables, a life of ease? Keep them!
My food is peace of mind, not rich rewards:
A food you'd choose yourself, if you were wise.
Men could call you Agamemnon's daughter,
Child of the noblest man who ever lived;
Instead, they call you Clytemnestra's child,
Who betrayed her father and everyone she loved.

FIRST WOMAN

My dears, no good will come of quarrelling.
Listen to each other: listen and learn.

CHRYSOTHEMIS

I'm used to the way she speaks to me.
I'd never have begun this argument
Except for my dreadful news. Disaster
Is coming, to stop her complaints forever.

ELECTRA

Disaster? What disaster? Tell me.
What could be worse than what I suffer now?

ELECTRA
A coward's thought. Hug it for comfort!

CHRYSOTHEMIS
Electra, listen! Follow my advice.

ELECTRA
Follow you – and give up what sense I have?

CHRYSOTHEMIS
There's no more to say. I must go now.

ELECTRA
Where must you go? What offerings are those?

CHRYSOTHEMIS
Our mother's, sent for our father's grave.

ELECTRA
Offerings – from her? To the man she hated?

CHRYSOTHEMIS
To the man she killed. Say what you mean.

ELECTRA
Who persuaded her to make him offerings?

CHRYSOTHEMIS
I think she was sent a warning, in a dream.

ELECTRA
O gods of Argos, come down to me now!

CHRYSOTHEMIS
You mean this dream, this warning, gives you hope?

ELECTRA
Tell me the dream, and I'll know for sure.

CHRYSOTHEMIS
I know no details. There's little to tell.

ELECTRA
Tell me what there is. A single word
Can be the word of fate, for good or ill.

CHRYSOTHEMIS
This is all I know. Our father came:
She saw him in front of her, restored to life.
He took the staff of the kings of Argos,
That once was his, and now Aegisthus holds,
And planted it in the earth beside the hearth.
At once it grew and blossomed, a green tree
Whose branches overshadowed all Mycenae.
That was the dream; I heard it from a slave
Who was by her side when she told it

At the altar of Helios, god of the sun.
No more than that: she was terrified,
And gave me these offerings for Agamemnon's grave.
Electra, I beg you, listen!
If you destroy yourself, I cannot help!

ELECTRA

Chrysothemis – sister – these offerings:
Make none of them. The gods will not allow
Gifts from that witch-wife to touch our father's grave.
He is sleeping: scatter them on the breeze,
Or bury them deep. They must not reach him.
When she dies, she'll find them waiting,
Mementoes of what she did. I tell you,
She's the most shameless woman left alive,
To send garlands of hate to the man she killed!
Does she imagine the corpse will smile his thanks,
His gratitude – to the enemy who killed him?
She butchered him: hacked at his lifeless corpse
And wiped the sword-blade clean in his own hair –
Is her guilt to be wiped away so easily
By these grave-gifts? Do you think that?
No! Throw them away. Instead, offer him
A lock of your hair. And give him these gifts
From me: poor gifts, but they are all I have.
A twist of hair – dull, not glossy like yours –
And this plain cloth belt. Go down on your knees
And beg him to rise from the grave
And help us. Beg him to bring Orestes home,
A strong arm, a foot to trample our enemies.
When we have won, we'll garland the grave
With richer gifts than any we give him now.

Do you understand, Chrysothemis? I think
Our father sent the dream that frightened her.
But even if he did not, do as I ask:
Do it for my sake, for yours, and for his –
Our dear father, who lies with the dead below.

FIRST WOMAN

My child, do as she asks. She speaks
With a daughter's love. Help her, do as she asks.

CHRYSOTHEMIS

Yes. I'll do it, and do it at once.

My duty is clear, and needs no arguing.
Only . . . if you are my friends, I beg you
By all the gods, help me, keep it secret:
If our mother finds out what I have done,
What I have dared, my tears will be the price.

She hurries out.

WOMEN

Am I wise? Do I understand?
Was this an omen, sent
By Justice the Avenger?
Soon, my child,
She will come down to us
And bring the strength we need.
When we heard that dream
A breeze of hope
Stirred in our hearts.
Your father, warlord of the Greeks,
Has not abandoned you;
The axe, the double axe,
The butcher's bronze
That showed no mercy then
Will show none now.

The avenging Furies hide,
Waiting to pounce –
They are an army
Marching in bronze;
They are monsters of doom
Who sniff the murderers out,
The lecherous, unlawful lust,
The butchers, coupling in blood.
A breeze of hope
Stirs in our hearts.
Was Agamemnon's ghost
Glimpsed in the night
A true omen? If not,
All dreams, all prophecies,
Wither and die.

For the house of Pelops
A chariot-race long ago

Began the line of death.
The prize was marriage,
The king's own daughter's hand;
And Pelops won the race.
For Myrtilus, who challenged him,
Disaster came, and death.
Hurled headlong from the golden car,
Cheated and tricked,
He drowned in the roaring sea:
An evil omen
For Pelops and all his line.
Now misery and death
Still haunt this house.[3]

They draw back, as the palace doors are opened and CLYTEMNESTRA *comes out. She, too, is carrying grave-gifts. When she sees* ELECTRA, *she goes angrily to her.*

CLYTEMNESTRA
Still you go freely, anywhere you choose!
If he was here, Aegisthus would keep you
Indoors, where you'd bring us no disgrace.
But he's away, and you pay no heed to me,
Although you cry to the whole world
That I'm a tyrant, crushing you alive.
How am I harming you? With these hard words?
They are no harder than your words to me.

You talk of nothing but your father.
You say I caused his death – and I admit it.
What you say is true. I caused his death –
In Justice's name. The criminal paid –
In Justice's name. I helped – as you
Should have helped – in Justice's name.
This father of yours, the father you mourn,
Did what no other Greek has ever dared:
He took his own daughter, Iphigenia,
Your sister, and sacrificed her to the gods.
His own child! Her begetting caused him no pain,
Compared to mine when I gave her birth.

Why should he kill her? For the Greeks?
They had no right to take a child of mine.
For his brother Menelaus' sake?
If that was his excuse, he deserved his death.
Menelaus had two children of his own –
They should have died before my daughter.
Their father and mother began the Trojan War.
Was it some hunger of the king of Hades,
Greed for my daughter's flesh, not theirs?
The children of Menelaus! Were they
The only ones your father ever loved?

He was callous and cruel, a murderer.
How can you deny it? Your own sister
Iphigenia would say so, if the dead could speak.
I caused his death, Electra – and I'm glad,
Not sorry. Before you call me a criminal,
Consider who is right and who is wrong.

ELECTRA

I've said nothing, this time,
To deserve such angry words.
Will you let me answer, let me say what must
Be said, for my father's and sister's sake?

CLYTEMNESTRA

Speak. It's allowed. If you always began
With such respect, I'd be glad to hear.

ELECTRA

I have this to say. You admit that you killed
My father. Just or unjust, right or wrong,
That was a monstrous crime. And I say
That it was wrong: you were snared by Aegisthus' charms.
That criminal! The man you bed with now!
Ask the hunting-goddess, ask Artemis,
What sin made her hold back the winds
At Aulis. No, *I* will tell you:
No mortal must question a god.
This is the story. Agamemnon was hunting
In her sacred wood; his footsteps startled
A dappled, antlered stag – her sacred stag.
He took aim, and killed it. The stag's death

And the hunter's triumph angered Artemis.
She held back the wind, becalmed the fleet.
The price for the deer, the price she set
For a wind, was Agamemnon's daughter's life.
Only her sacrifice would unlock the fleet
And give them fair sailing, for home or Troy.
He did no favour for Menelaus.
He was forced to kill her. He had no choice.

But even if it had been a favour, even if
You were right, and he murdered his own child
To gratify his brother – would that give you
The right to murder him? Blood for blood –
Is that your law? If so, you condemn yourself:
You murdered; now you must die.

But you're wrong. These are empty words.
Do they explain the worst sin of all?
You sleep with a murderer, the man
Who helped you kill my father;
You sleep with him, and make new children
To take the place of those you have driven out.
What excuse can you give for that?
Is it revenge for Iphigenia's death –
Was this monstrous marriage made to avenge her death?
Is that what you say? Is that what you call just?

You refuse to listen to me;
You scream that I'm insolent,
Impertinent to my mother. Mother!
Jailer, I call you. I live
No better than a slave; I'm heaped
With insults by you and your . . . bedmate.
And Orestes too, Orestes who escaped you,
Is fretting away his life in exile.
You blame me for that: you say
I saved him to punish you one day.
If only I had! If only I could!
Call me what names you like: wild,
Shameless, impertinent. My answer is
That it's true, I am all of them:
My mother's true daughter in every way.

FIRST WOMAN
She's furious – too furious to care
Whether what she says is right or wrong.

CLYTEMNESTRA
But I care. She's not a child.
You hear the way she speaks
To her own mother. Is there more to come?
Fresh insolence? Is she not ashamed?

ELECTRA
Ashamed? Of course I'm ashamed,
Whatever you choose to think. Remember:
If I go too far, if I forget myself,
The fault is yours. Your treatment
Forces me to answer hate with hate.
Evil breeds evil – I learned from you.

CLYTEMNESTRA
That's enough! Such insolence! You talk
Too much of what I do and what I say.

ELECTRA
No! Your own words, your own actions,
Speak for themselves. They need no words from me.

CLYTEMNESTRA
Artemis, queen of heaven! When Aegisthus
Comes home, you'll suffer for this.

ELECTRA
You see? You allow me to speak, and then
You lose your temper and refuse to hear.

CLYTEMNESTRA
I've heard enough, allowed enough!
Now hold your tongue, and let me sacrifice.

ELECTRA
Yes, sacrifice. I'll hold my tongue.
I've said my say: there is nothing more.

CLYTEMNESTRA
Slave, bring forward the offerings.
I'll pray now; I'll ask
Lord Apollo to free me from these fears.

She goes to the altar. While a SLAVE *sees to the offerings, she prays.* ELECTRA *has turned away.*

Apollo! Protector! Hear and answer
The prayers I speak, and the secret prayers
Locked in my heart. I dare not
Unveil my thoughts while she is here,
My enemy, standing beside me,
A malicious tongue, eager as ever
For gossip to scatter in the town.
Hear my words, and hear my hidden thoughts.

Lycean Apollo, I dreamed of a ghost
In the night, a vision with no clear meaning.
If the omen is good, fulfil it;
If it's bad, turn it aside,
Turn it against my enemies.
They are plotting to hurl me down
From the rich seat of power. Prevent them!
Grant me forever unbroken peace,
Unbroken power in the house of Atreus.
Let me live a life of love with those
Who love me, with all of my children
Whose minds are not sick with bitter hate.

Hear me, Apollo! Grant these prayers,
For mine and the city's sake. Fulfil
The words I speak, the wishes of my heart.
You understand my secret prayers,
For nothing is hidden from the son of Zeus.

She stays kneeling by the altar. Orestes' old SERVANT *comes in, pretending to be a traveller uncertain of the way.*

SERVANT
Ladies . . . I wonder, can you tell me
If this is the palace of Lord Aegisthus?

FIRST WOMAN
Yes, sir. You have found it. This is the place.

SERVANT
And that royal lady . . . there by the altar . . .
Is that Clytemnestra? Is that the queen?

FIRST WOMAN
You are in the presence of the queen herself.

CLYTEMNESTRA rises, and the SERVANT goes to her.

SERVANT
Your Majesty, I come from friends, with news –
Good news, for Lord Aegisthus and yourself.

CLYTEMNESTRA
An omen from heaven! I welcome it.
What news, sir? Where are you from?

SERVANT
I was sent by Phanoteus of Phocis.

CLYTEMNESTRA
An old friend. You bring good news
From a good friend. What is it? Speak.

SERVANT
Orestes is dead. Just that, no more.

ELECTRA
O gods! Orestes – ? How can I bear it?

CLYTEMNESTRA
Again! Again! Ignore her. Tell me again.

SERVANT
He's dead, my lady. Orestes is dead.

ELECTRA
Zeus! Zeus! Will you not kill me too?

CLYTEMNESTRA
Be quiet. Leave us in peace. And you, sir,
Tell me in detail, exactly how he died.

SERVANT
Yes, my lady. It was for that I was sent.
Orestes had gone to the Pythian Games
In Delphi, the best in Greece. The Games began,
And heralds announced the opening event:
A footrace. Orestes stood up to take part,
A dazzling figure, admired by everyone.
He ran the race; his performance matched
His appearance; he won the victor's crown.

After that, what can I say? To cut it short,
No other competitor could match him.
Whatever competition was announced –
Sprinting, distance, pentathlon – he won with ease,

And stood smiling while the victor's name was called:
'Orestes, son of Agamemnon, son
Of the general who once commanded Greece.'

So far, so good. But when a god sends harm,
What man can escape, however fine and strong?
The day for the chariot-race arrived.
It was a fast event, and began at dawn.
Ten competitors moved to the starting-line:
An Achaean, a Spartan, and next to them
Two drivers from Cyrene, skilful and fast.
Orestes was fifth in line, driving a team
Of mares from Thessaly; an Aetolian sixth,
With chestnut colts; a Magnesian seventh;
The eighth, an Aenian, was driving bays;
The ninth was from Athens, founded by the gods,
And a Boeotian, tenth, completed the line.

So they waited in line, each chariot
Keeping well inside its allotted place.
The trumpet blared, and they were off. Each man
Shouted to his horses, and shook the reins;
The pounding of hooves and rattle of chariots
Filled all the course; dust billowed to the sky.

For the first few laps they were tightly bunched.
There was no mercy: they goaded their horses on.
Each driver tried to inch his chariot past
His opponent's wheels, his opponent's team.
The horses were snorting foam; flecked with its drops
They hurtled on, neck and neck, wheel by flying wheel.

To begin with, none of them overturned.
Then, suddenly, on the turn from the sixth
To the seventh laps, the Aenian's horses took
The bit between their teeth; they swerved across
The course, head-on into one of the teams
From Cyrene. After that, crash followed crash
As driver after driver bit the dust.
The course was a battlefield, choked with wrecks.

The Athenian driver, an old hand,
Had seen this danger coming. He drew in

And let the sea of hooves and wheels go by,
Surging up the centre of the track. Orestes
Had stayed behind him, keeping his mares fresh
For a victory-gallop in the final lap.
When he saw that only the Athenian
Was left to beat, he shouted to his team
And gave chase. Neck and neck they pounded on;
First one, then the other, inched ahead.

Orestes was on the inside. Each time he passed
The turning-post at the end of the lap,
His axle almost grazed it; just in time, each time,
He pulled to the right, and gave his horses rein.
He made the turn each time, with no damage
To himself or his chariot. So far, so good.
But then, on the last lap, he misjudged the turn,
Slipped rein too soon, and hit the turning-post.
The axle splintered, and Orestes was hurled
Across the driver's handrail to the ground.
He was tangled in broken reins; his horses
Bolted, and dragged him feet first across the course.

The crowd groaned in sympathy to see him fall –
So many triumphs, such a dreadful end.
He was smashed on the ground, tossed headlong
In the air. At last, after a struggle, grooms
Managed to control the runaways, and cut
His mangled body free: torn, oozing blood,
Hard even for his friends to recognise.

They burned the corpse at once, on a funeral pyre.
And now a burial-party is coming here
From Phocis, bringing his ashes – so great
A man, poor ashes in a little urn! –
To be laid to rest in his native land.

Your Majesty, that is my story – sad
To hear, but for those of us who saw it
The worst disaster our eyes have ever seen.[4]

FIRST WOMAN

The last shoot of the royal house, destroyed!
The dynasty of Argos has withered and died.

CLYTEMNESTRA
O Zeus! Is this the news I longed to hear,
The pain that sets me free? Can I be glad
To be safe at last, by my own son's death?

SERVANT
My lady, why does this news distress you so?

CLYTEMNESTRA
I was his mother. However she is wronged,
A mother never hates the child she bore.

SERVANT
Then I was wrong to tell you, wrong to come?

CLYTEMNESTRA
Wrong? No. How could it be wrong to bring me proof,
Clear proof that he is dead? He was my own son,
Flesh of my flesh. He tore himself away
From his own mother's milk; he went into exile,
A stranger, far from home. From that day on
He held me guilty of Agamemnon's death;
He swore vengeance; he snatched my sleep away;
Night and day, I knew I was marked for death.

And now, today, you tell me he is dead.
I am free of fear at last: fear of my son,
And fear of that thirsty one who lives with me,
Drinking my life. Now her brother is dead,
I can ignore her threats. I can live in peace.

ELECTRA
O Orestes, my poor Orestes!
To die as you died, and now to be mocked
By your own mother! How you are suffering!

CLYTEMNESTRA
No: you are suffering. His sufferings are done.

ELECTRA
Avenging Furies, do you hear her now?

CLYTEMNESTRA
They heard me then: heard me and judged the case.

ELECTRA
Yes, gloat! Insult us! Enjoy your victory!

CLYTEMNESTRA
You'll not stop me, then – either of you?

ELECTRA
We have been stopped. We can't stop you now.

CLYTEMNESTRA
Do you hear that, my friend? Your journey here
Deserves a rich reward: you've stopped her tongue.

SERVANT
There's no more to say. May I go now?

CLYTEMNESTRA
Go now? Before I have shown my gratitude
To yourself and my good friend who sent you here?
Come inside. Leave her out here, squealing
Her sorrows, and the fate of those she loved.

She takes him into the palace.

ELECTRA
Did you see how she suffered? Did you see
Her agonies of grief for the son she lost?
She laughed, and left. O Orestes, Orestes,
My darling, your death is my death too.
You have torn from my heart the last rags of hope –
That you would come home, to punish them
For my father's death and what they have done to me.
Where must I turn now? I have no one:
He is dead, and you are dead. Must I go inside
And bow to them again, the masters I hate,
My father's butchers? Must I suffer that?

I'll never go in again. I'll lie down,
Here at the gate, and starve to death, alone.
And if they see me, if they are angry,
Let them kill me – for charity, kill me now.
What use is my life to me? It is agony.

The lament that follows is accompanied by music and choral movement.

WOMEN
Where are Zeus' thunderbolts?
Where is the fiery Sun?
Are they sleeping? Why
Do they not scorch this guilt?

ELECTRA (*wordless sobs*)
Ah . . . ah . . .
FIRST WOMAN
My poor child . . .
ELECTRA
No . . . no . . .
FIRST WOMAN
Don't cry. Hush, child.
No more weeping.
ELECTRA
You are breaking my heart.
FIRST WOMAN
How?
ELECTRA
They are in Hades; they have gone
Down to the underworld forever.
Will you still offer me hope?
Leave me. Leave me to weep.
FIRST WOMAN
There was King Amphiaraus:[5]
Snared by a woman
For a necklace of gold;
And now, in the underworld . . .
ELECTRA (*sobbing*)
Ah . . . ah . . .
FIRST WOMAN
He rules among the dead.
ELECTRA
No . . . no . . .
FIRST WOMAN
And the woman,
The murderess . . .
ELECTRA
Paid with her life?
FIRST WOMAN
Yes.
ELECTRA
Yes! A champion rose up
To avenge his death.
Where is my champion?
He is snatched away and gone.

FIRST WOMAN
Your life is cruel and hard.

ELECTRA
I have borne all there is to bear.
Whirlpools of grief,
Unending misery.

FIRST WOMAN
We have seen your suffering.

ELECTRA
Leave me to suffer, then.
Do not flatter me –

FIRST WOMAN
How?

ELECTRA
By offering empty hope:
My brother, my royal father's son.

FIRST WOMAN
All men must die one day.

ELECTRA
Like him? Like poor Orestes?
In a tangle of reins,
A trampling of hooves?

FIRST WOMAN
A bitter sight to see.

ELECTRA
A bitter death. Far
From home, far away –

FIRST WOMAN
Far . . .

ELECTRA
In a stranger's grave
Unwept, unmourned.

As the lament ends, CHRYSOTHEMIS *runs in, full of excitement.*

CHRYSOTHEMIS
Electra! My dear, my darling Electra!
I picked up my skirts, and ran all the way
To tell you. Wonderful news! The end
Of all your suffering, the end of your grief!

ELECTRA
My grief, my suffering, are past all cure.
No news is wonderful. No news can help.

CHRYSOTHEMIS
Orestes is here! He has come back to us!
I know it, as sure as I am standing here.

ELECTRA
Are you insane? How can you be so cruel?
Must you laugh at your own unhappiness, and mine?

CHRYSOTHEMIS
I swear by the gods of Argos, it's true.
This is no mockery. Orestes is back.

ELECTRA
No. You're wrong. What made you think so?
Has someone told you this, persuaded you?

CHRYSOTHEMIS
I know it for myself, from no one else.
I saw clear proof: I saw, with my own eyes.

ELECTRA
What proof did you see? You're on fire,
Blazing with hope. What proof did you see?

CHRYSOTHEMIS
Just listen, Electra! Then, when I've done,
See if you still think me insane. Listen!

ELECTRA
Tell me, then, if telling brings you joy.

CHRYSOTHEMIS
This is what happened. When I went just now
To take the offerings to our father's grave,
I saw that the top of the mound was wet
With a grave-gift of milk, and there were flowers,
All kinds of flowers, round it in wreaths.
I stood there amazed. I looked all round,
In case anyone was near. But the whole place
Was deserted and still. I crept nearer,
Up to the grave. There, lying on the edge,
There was another offering: a lock
Of hair, newly cut off. As soon as I saw it,
My whole being filled with thoughts of him:
Orestes our brother, dearest of men.

I picked it up; I could say nothing;
My eyes were blurred with tears. I know,
Electra, I know now as I knew then,
That Orestes is here. These offerings
Are his, they can have come from no one else.
Only you or I ever visit the grave.
I did not leave them. You could not have gone:
If you leave the palace yard, even to pray,
They punish you. Was it our mother? No!
Why should she choose to go? And even if
She had, she would have said, we would have known.

No. They can only have come from Orestes.
Take heart, Electra! Our luck must change.
Until now, sorrow and pain; but from today
Unending joy, unending happiness!

ELECTRA
Fool! Do you know nothing? I pity you.

CHRYSOTHEMIS
What is it? Does what I say not please you?

ELECTRA
You know nothing. You're in a world of dreams.

CHRYSOTHEMIS
What more should I know? I know what I saw!

ELECTRA
You fool, he's dead. Orestes is dead.
He can do nothing to help us. Forget him.

CHRYSOTHEMIS
How do you know? Who told you he was dead?

ELECTRA
A man who was there, who saw him die.

CHRYSOTHEMIS
I can't believe it. Where is he now?

ELECTRA
In the palace – our mother's welcome guest.

CHRYSOTHEMIS
But if he is dead – Orestes – who left
The offerings? Who visited the grave?

ELECTRA
A stranger, perhaps: a pious stranger
Who left them to honour Orestes' death.

CHRYSOTHEMIS
To think I ran to bring you such good news!
How could I know, how could I understand
This new burden of grief, new misery
To add to the old? Electra, how could I know?

ELECTRA
You understand at last. Now, listen to me.
There's still a way for you to ease our grief.

CHRYSOTHEMIS
How can there be? Must I bring the dead to life?

ELECTRA
It's foolish to think so. There are other ways.

CHRYSOTHEMIS
If only I have the strength. What must I do?

ELECTRA
Be brave, and do exactly as I say.

CHRYSOTHEMIS
If I can help, I'll do what I can.

ELECTRA
Remember, to win we must be prepared to fight.

CHRYSOTHEMIS
I understand. I'll not refuse to help.

ELECTRA
Listen, then. These are my hopes, my plans.
First, you must realise we are alone –
Our dear ones have been snatched by the lord of death,
And only we are left. There is no one else.
While Orestes was alive, and safe, I had hopes
That one day he would come back to Argos
And punish the murderers. But he is dead,
And I must turn to you, Chrysothemis.
Will you help your sister? Will you nerve yourself
To butcher that butcher, that criminal,
Aegisthus? There. Nothing is hidden now.

Think. Will you help me, or do nothing still?
What else can you cling to? Your hope is dead.
Only grief is left, grief that you have lost
A noble father, a rich inheritance,
Grief that your life is withering away
With no husband, no children and no hope.

Yes! You can put away all marriage-thoughts –
Unless you think Aegisthus such a fool
That he would let a child of yours or mine
Be born, grow up and live – to murder him.

All your hope is in me, Chrysothemis.
If you help me, if you do as I ask,
You will be honoured by the dead below –
Our father, our brother. You will be free,
No longer a slave; you will be a child
Worthy of Agamemnon; a prince's bride.

Help me, and these are the names you will win.
The citizens of Argos, and strangers too,
Will greet us with honour. 'Look,' they will say,
'There go the sisters who saved the royal house;
They turned on a triumphant enemy
And cut him down; they avenged their father's death.
They have the courage of men, not women:
Sing them hymns of praise, and celebrate
Their bravery, the glory of their name.'

Our courage will be known over all the world.
Alive or dead, we'll be remembered, always.
Do as I ask, Chrysothemis! Be brave
And fight, for our father's and brother's sake.
Leave cowardice to cowards! Arm yourself
To end our weakness, our suffering, for evermore.

FIRST WOMAN

My children, it's time for caution.
Speak well; listen well. Do nothing rash.

CHRYSOTHEMIS

Caution? My friends, she's out of her mind.
You heard what she intends to do; you heard
Her ask me to help. Where is caution in that?

You have no power, Electra. Your only weapon
Is rashness. How can I help? How can you hope
To win? You're a woman, not a man.
You're weak, and your enemies are strong.
The gods favour them; their strength grows day by day;
Ours withers and shrinks away. Kings in their power!
If you challenge them, you'll destroy yourself.

When Aegisthus gets to hear these plans of yours,
He'll punish us both, with punishments
Worse than all we suffer now. You say
We shall win glory and honour. What good is that
If we die like criminals – or worse than that,
If they make us live, if they'll not let us die?

Give up your anger. You're destroying us.
The last survivors of the royal house –
Must we die too? I beg you, Electra,
Give up your anger. The words you said
Can be unsaid, forgotten – I'll see to that.
But you must give way; you must realise
At last that you are weak and they are strong.
Admit it! Bow to the king and queen!

FIRST WOMAN
My child, do as she says. The greatest gifts
In human life are caution and common sense.

ELECTRA
You say nothing unexpected. I knew
You'd refuse: there was no need to ask.
It's there, it must be done. I must do it.
If no one will help, I must do it alone.

CHRYSOTHEMIS
And what of the day they killed our father –
And you did nothing? Where was your courage then?

ELECTRA
How could I kill them then? I was too young.

CHRYSOTHEMIS
If you were too young then, be too young now!

ELECTRA
There's no more to say. You refuse to help.

CHRYSOTHEMIS
You'll destroy yourself. Of course I refuse.

ELECTRA
Wise coward! I admire you, and despise you too.

CHRYSOTHEMIS
One day you'll admit I was right. Till then –

ELECTRA
Till *then*? A day that will never come!

CHRYSOTHEMIS
No one can tell the future. We shall see.

ELECTRA
Go inside. I have finished now.
CHRYSOTHEMIS
If only you'd listen! If only you'd –
ELECTRA
Go inside. Tell your mother all you've heard.
CHRYSOTHEMIS
Electra! How can you think I hate you so?
ELECTRA
You despise me. You want me to give way.
CHRYSOTHEMIS
I want to save you. Is that despising you?
ELECTRA
And to be saved, I must do what you call right?
CHRYSOTHEMIS
It is right. Do it, and then I can help.
ELECTRA
You're so clever! So clever – and so wrong.
CHRYSOTHEMIS
It's you that's wrong. Why can't you understand?
ELECTRA
How is it wrong to fight for what is right?
CHRYSOTHEMIS
If you destroy yourself, then it is wrong.
ELECTRA
I'll never live with principles like that.
CHRYSOTHEMIS
If you attack the king, you'll see I was right.
ELECTRA
Whatever you say, I *shall* attack the king.
CHRYSOTHEMIS
Will nothing stop you? Will nothing change your mind?
ELECTRA
Change right for wrong? Courage for cowardice? No!
CHRYSOTHEMIS
You refuse to listen, whatever I say?
ELECTRA
I have made up my mind; I will never change.
CHRYSOTHEMIS
There's no more to say. You refuse to see
That all I'm asking is common sense;
I'll never agree that what you are doing is right.

ELECTRA
Go inside. We are walking separate paths.
However much you try, you'll not persuade me:
You are chasing shadows – a foolish task.

CHRYSOTHEMIS
Go ahead, then, if you think yourself so wise.
But when you've tried and failed, when you suffer,
You'll remember my words and agree at last.

She goes into the palace.

WOMEN
Look up, and see: birds of the air,
With tender devotion, protect and cherish
The adults who gave them life,
Who reared them. Why are we not the same?
Have we not the same debt to pay?
In the name of the thunderbolt of Zeus,
In the name of Justice, enthroned on high,
Where there is crime, there must be punishment.
O voice of the listening Dead,
Cry sorrow to them now,
The children of Atreus under the earth:
Cry bitterness and shame.

Tell them the sickness of the house;
Tell them of two sisters, once loving friends,
Now twisted enemies: all love,
All charity forgotten. Tell them, too,
How Electra is sailing the storm alone,
Weeping still for a father lost –
Like a nightingale: crying, crying . . .
Loyal Electra! How gladly
She would die, how gladly
She would leave the light of day,
If only she could snatch away
The twin monsters of the house.

Nobility of soul will never stoop
To live as cowards live,
Tarnished, dishonoured.
O my child, my child,
You have chosen this path,
The common path of grief.

You are armed against evil;
You are called loyal, and wise.

O gods, may we live to see
Agamemnon's daughter
Triumph against the enemies
Who trample her now!
Electra, child of misery,
You have honoured the laws
Of the gods, you have honoured Zeus:
You will destroy your enemies.

ORESTES *and* PYLADES *come in.* PYLADES *is carrying an urn.*

ORESTES
Ladies, I wonder . . . is this the place
We are looking for? Have we taken the right road?

FIRST WOMAN
What place, sir? Have you some business here?

ORESTES
I'm looking for King Aegisthus' house.

FIRST WOMAN
This is it. You have taken the right road.

ORESTES
Thank you. I wonder, would one of you go inside
And tell him we bring him longed-for news?

FIRST WOMAN (*indicating Electra*)
She'll do it. She's closest to them in blood.

ORESTES
Woman, go inside, if you will, and tell them
That we have come from Phocis to bring them news.

ELECTRA
O Zeus! Zeus! Is this the proof at last?
Clear proof that the story we heard was true?

ORESTES
I know nothing of stories. Strophios
Of Phocis sent me. It's about Orestes.

ELECTRA
Orestes? What? I am trembling with fear.

ORESTES
He's dead, lady. We've brought him home,
All that's left of him, in a little urn.

ELECTRA
How can I bear it? The story was true . . .
A burden of grief. You have brought him home.

ORESTES
If you're weeping for Orestes, he's here:
His ashes are all that's left, here in this urn.

ELECTRA
His ashes . . . here in this urn . . . all that is left.
Please let me hold it . . . in god's name . . .
I beg you, on my knees . . . let me hold it, and weep
For him, for me, and for all our stricken house.

ORESTES
Pylades, give her the urn, and let her weep.
Whoever she is, she loved Orestes once.
A friend, perhaps, or one of his own blood?

ELECTRA *takes the urn.*

ELECTRA
O ashes of Orestes, dust of the dearest of men!
Dear ashes, where are all the hopes
I had when I sent you away? Where are they now?
You were a torch of hope for all our house,
And now you are nothing, dust in my hands.
These hands sent you away, snatched you from death
And sent you abroad, to strangers. If only
The gods had prevented me! You would have died
With our father; you would have shared his death
And taken your place beside him in the grave.
But the gods did nothing, and now you have died
A wretched death abroad, among strangers,
Far from your sister's care. Whose loving hands
Washed clean your wounds? Who laid you on the fire,
Glowing coals weighted with grief?
They were strangers' hands, not mine:
Strangers tended you and brought you home,
Thin ashes in a little urn.

O Orestes, darling Orestes,
Do you remember how I cherished you?
You were my baby, not hers, not our mother's,
Not any of the nursemaids' in the palace.

'Sister,' you called me: I was the only one.
Now all that is gone, dead on the day you died.
Like dust on the wind, you have been snatched away.
Our father is dead; now you have left me too;
All I had is gone; let me die with you.

Do you hear how our enemies laugh? Do you see
How she dances for joy, the witch-mother
You promised one day to kill? Our black fate,
Orestes, stole that promise forever,
And sent me back, instead of my dear brother,
Dust, ash, a shadow of emptiness.

O my darling,
My dearest darling,
O Orestes,
You are walking a fearful path; and I am dead,
Dead in your death. Take me with you,
Nothing to nothing, inside the grave;
Let me lie with you there forever.
When you were here in the world above, we shared
Everything, you and I. Let me share your death!
Take me with you. There in the world below
Pain ends, and sorrow ends. The dead are at peace.

FIRST WOMAN
Electra, my child, remember. Your father
Was mortal. Orestes was mortal too.
Do not grieve too much for them. They have paid
The debt owed by all mortal men, to death.

ORESTES (*aside*)
Now, Pylades, what can I say? What words
Will help? I can keep silent no longer.

ELECTRA
What's the matter? What are you saying, sir?

ORESTES
Are you really Electra, princess Electra?

ELECTRA
Princess Electra, yes – princess of grief.

ORESTES
I am sorry for what has happened –

ELECTRA
You are sorry? Sorry for whom? For me?

ORESTES
Treated so cruelly, abandoned by the gods –

ELECTRA
These are words of ill omen, but they are true.

ORESTES
Kept without a husband, treated like a slave –

ELECTRA
Sir, we are strangers. Why do you grieve for me?

ORESTES
For you? For me! I understand at last.

ELECTRA
My words have made you understand?

ORESTES
Your words, yes, and the suffering I see.

ELECTRA
The suffering you see! If that was all – !

ORESTES
There is worse than this? Is that what you mean?

ELECTRA
Day and night I must live with murderers.

ORESTES
What murderers? And who was murdered? Speak.

ELECTRA
They murdered my father, and made me a slave.

ORESTES
You must name them, Electra: name the criminals.

ELECTRA
Her name is: mother. The name is all she has.

ORESTES
How does she ill-treat you? Does she beat you? Starve you?

ELECTRA
She is wicked and cruel in everything she does.

ORESTES
Will no one help you, no one take your part?

ELECTRA
There was one, once. You brought his ashes home.

ORESTES
Unhappy Electra! I pity you –

ELECTRA
If you pity me, you are alone on earth.

ORESTES
Yes – alone on earth, I share your suffering.
ELECTRA
You share it? How? Are you a distant kinsman – ?
ORESTES
I would say more . . . These women: can I trust them?
ELECTRA
They are good friends. You can trust them. Speak.
ORESTES
If you give me back the urn, I will explain.
ELECTRA
No! No! I beg you, don't ask me that.
ORESTES
Do as I ask. No harm will come of it.
ELECTRA
My brother's ashes . . . they're all I have . . .
ORESTES
Give me the urn.

He takes the urn.

ELECTRA
O Orestes, darling Orestes,
You are stolen away, cheated of burial . . .
ORESTES
Enough. There's no need to talk of burial.
ELECTRA
No need . . . ? When my brother is dead?
ORESTES
That's not the way to think of him now.
ELECTRA
Does my dear dead brother reject me too?
ORESTES
No one rejects you. There is no need to mourn.
ELECTRA
But his ashes . . . I held them in my hands.
ORESTES
Those were not his ashes. It was a lie.
ELECTRA
Where is he buried, then? Where is his grave?

ORESTES
He has no grave. The living have no graves.
ELECTRA
The living? Oh . . . ! You say –
ORESTES
It's the truth.
ELECTRA
Orestes is alive?
ORESTES
As *I* live, *he* lives.
ELECTRA
You are Orestes?
ORESTES
Look, Electra:
Our father's ring . . . Agamemnon's ring. Look.
ELECTRA
O my dear . . . my darling . . .
ORESTES
Electra . . . sister . . .
ELECTRA
Your dear voice . . . you have come home . . .
ORESTES
I have come home.
ELECTRA
Let me hold you . . . kiss you . . . forever . . .
ORESTES
Forever.
ELECTRA
O my dear friends, women of Argos, look:
Orestes died, they said, and it was a trick –
Now another trick, and he's alive again.
FIRST WOMAN
We see him, child; and for this happiness
Tears of relief and joy run down our cheeks.
ELECTRA
O my brother,
My dear father's son,
Suddenly, beyond all hope,
You have come, you are home.
ORESTES
Electra, hush –

ELECTRA
What is it?
ORESTES
They'll hear inside.
ELECTRA
By Artemis
Queen of heaven,
I'll never fear them
Again, those women,
Those parasites, inside.
ORESTES
Remember: Ares the war-god lives
In women too – as you have seen.
ELECTRA
Do not speak of it!
The grief, the misery
That tortures me
Endlessly, beyond all cure.
ORESTES
The time will come.
We'll remember, and punish them.
ELECTRA
I must speak!
In Justice's name
I must tell my suffering.
We're safe now: let me speak.
ORESTES
Electra, soon –
ELECTRA
When? When?
ORESTES
Soon will be time: not now.
ELECTRA
Now you are home –
Beyond hope or thought
You are home. Who
Would keep silent now?
Who would not shout for joy?
ORESTES
The gods spoke. The time has come.
The murderers must pay the price.

ELECTRA
Sing, then, for joy!
If the gods have spoken,
If the gods have brought you home
To Argos, sing for joy!

ORESTES
Electra, hush! When the murderers
Are punished, it will be time to sing.

ELECTRA
I waited, I watched
Your dear road home.
At last you came:
The long misery is done.
O Orestes, never leave me,
Never leave me again.

ORESTES
No one will part us now.

ELECTRA
Do you swear it?

ORESTES
Forever.

ELECTRA (*to the* WOMEN)
O my friends, when I heard
My brother's voice, the dear voice
I thought never to hear again,
How could I not sing for joy?
He has come home, my dear one,
My darling, the brother I longed for.

ORESTES
Say no more now. Tell me later
The story of all our mother's crimes,
How Aegisthus squanders the royal wealth
And sucks the storehouse dry. Tell me later:
There is too much to hear, and time is short.

Tell me this, now: just this I need to know.
How can we best attack them? Openly,
Or secretly, lying in wait, to put
An end to their smiling for evermore?

When Pylades and I have gone inside,
Your job will be to trick our mother. Hide

Your smiles of happiness, or she will know.
You must weep tears, tears for the dreadful news.
When we have succeeded, then you can smile.

ELECTRA

Dearest brother, you know I'm in your hands.
What you want, I want. You're all
My happiness; without you there is none.
I would not hurt you, not for all the world.
The gods are helping us. Our time is now.

You must know how things are in Argos:
Aegisthus is away, and our mother rules.
Our mother! I'll trick her, never fear.
No smiles, no happiness: I'll remember
The hate that has eaten my life away,
And I'll show her tears. Look, Orestes,
They are tears of joy. In a single day
You have come home to Argos twice, first dead
And now alive. For me, it is like
A miracle. If Father came back
And stood beside me now, I'd say
He was really there, he was not a ghost.
That's how you, now, appear to me. Tell me
What I must do to help. When you were dead,
And I was alone, I would have made my choice
A glorious victory or a glorious death.

ORESTES

Be quiet now. Someone's coming. I can hear them
There at the palace door.

ELECTRA

Go inside.
You bring them misery, not joy –
And it is a gift they cannot refuse.

Orestes' SERVANT *hurries to them from the palace.*

SERVANT

Orestes, Electra! You're like little children!
Are you tired of living? Have you lost
What common sense you had? You're in danger,
Deadly danger – not soon, but here and now.
Can't you see it? If I had not been here,

Keeping watch at the door, your words, your plans,
Would have been inside the palace before you.
You have me to thank for preventing it.
Have done with your speeches, your endless cries
Of joy. There's work to be done. Delay now
Will be fatal. Go inside, and finish it.

ORESTES

And when I'm inside, what will I find?

SERVANT

It's safe. No one will recognise you.

ORESTES

You've convinced them, then, that I am dead?

SERVANT

They all believe it: you are dead and gone.

ORESTES

What did they say? Were they glad to hear it?

SERVANT

When it's done, I'll tell you. As things are now,
They think they are safe, and they ask no more.

ELECTRA

Orestes, please tell me, who is this man?

ORESTES

Don't you recognise him?

ELECTRA

Not clearly, no.

ORESTES

He's the man you chose to save my life.

ELECTRA

To save . . . ? You mean – ?

ORESTES

Long ago, you made him
Take me to Phocis, to a safe hiding-place.

ELECTRA

This is the same man? The only man in Argos
Loyal to our father on the day he died?

ORESTES

The same man: no need of proof.

ELECTRA

O dearest of men! Our saviour, the saviour
Of Agamemnon's house, have you come home at last?
Is it really you? You have saved our lives;

You have ended our misery forever.
God bless the hands and feet that helped us so!
You were here, beside me in the palace,
And you gave me no sign: you broke my heart
With false stories, when all the time
You were bringing the news I longed to hear.
O let me embrace you, let me call you father –
My dear friend, on this one day
Most hated and dearest of men to me.

SERVANT

No more now. For all that has happened,
Electra, there will be many nights and days
To tell the story. Now, we must act.
Orestes and Pylades, the time is now:
The queen is alone, no soldiers are near.
Delay now, and you'll have to face
An army of guards, well-trained and well-armed.

ORESTES

Come inside, Pylades. The talking, the planning,
Is done. It's time. The gods are watching,
The guardians of Argos, here at the gate.
We honour them, and ask them to help us now.

He and PYLADES *go inside the palace.*

ELECTRA

Lord Apollo, hear them; grant their prayers.
I'm your servant; I've given you
What gifts I had. Apollo, hear me now.
On my knees I beg you,
Beseech you to help us.
Smile on us. Make our plans come true.
The gods have set a price on human wickedness:
Show all men, now, how it is paid!

She goes to the palace doors.

WOMEN

Ares the hunter, the war-god, is here.
He pants for blood. There is no escape.
Furies pad through the palace halls.
They have the scent. There is no escape.
The vision of hope

That fluttered in my heart
Lives: it will soon come true.

Orestes, champion of the dead, is here,
Stealthy inside the palace halls,
His father's rich palace of old.
Hermes, shepherd of souls,
Whispered secret ways.
It is not soon: it is now!

ELECTRA *comes back down to them.*

ELECTRA
Hush, women; hush, friends. Listen:
The men are at work. It is now.
FIRST WOMAN
What's happening? Tell us . . . tell us.
ELECTRA
She is preparing the urn for burial.
They are beside her. It is now.
FIRST WOMAN
Why are you not inside, to help?
ELECTRA
I must stand on guard;
I must watch for Aegisthus.
CLYTEMNESTRA (*a sudden scream, inside*)
Ah! Assassins! Help me!
Is there no one to help me?
ELECTRA
Inside. She's screaming. Can you hear?
FIRST WOMAN
We hear the death-cry;
We hear, and shudder.
CLYTEMNESTRA
Oh . . . oh! Aegisthus, help me!
ELECTRA
Another cry.
CLYTEMNESTRA
My son, O my son! Have pity . . .
ELECTRA
Yes! As you pitied him!
As you pitied his father!

FIRST WOMAN
People of Argos, children of Atreus,
The ancient curse is lifted, lifted.

CLYTEMNESTRA
Ah!

ELECTRA
Three blows. The laws demand three blows.

CLYTEMNESTRA
Ah!

ELECTRA
We must wait for Aegisthus now.

WOMEN
The curse is a living thing:
Dead men rise from the grave,
Dead men of old, to drink
The blood of those who murdered them.

FIRST WOMAN
Look: they are here. Crimson hands . . .
A sacrifice. The debt is paid.

ORESTES *and* PYLADES *come in, bloodstained, with drawn swords.*

ELECTRA
Orestes . . .

ORESTES
It is all right. Inside, it is all right,
If Apollo's prophecy is kept.

ELECTRA
The . . . woman . . . is dead?

ORESTES
Our mother is dead. Her pride,
Her cruelty . . . forget your fear.

FIRST WOMAN
My children, look: Aegisthus
Is coming. He is here.

ELECTRA
Orestes, Pylades, hurry . . .

ORESTES
Where is he? Can you see him?

FIRST WOMAN
Yes: he's coming up from the town.
He's smiling . . . he suspects nothing.
ELECTRA
Go back inside; wait for him there.
The gods helped you before – pray
That they are near to help you now.
ORESTES
Never fear: we're ready.
ELECTRA
Leave all the rest to me.

ORESTES *and* PYLADES *go into the palace.*

FIRST WOMAN
Honey his ears with words
To welcome a royal king;
Let him suspect nothing
Till Justice's trap is sprung.

AEGISTHUS *comes in from the side.*

AEGISTHUS
Where are the strangers from Phocis?
The ones who brought news of Orestes' death
In a shipwreck of chariots. Answer me.
You! Yes, you. Electra. Where are they?
What? Silent? You had so much to say before.
Tell me. He was your brother: you must know.
ELECTRA
Of course I know. My own brother – the brother
I loved more than all the world! Of course I know.
AEGISTHUS
Answer me, then. Where are the strangers from Phocis?
ELECTRA
Inside, with the queen. They went straight to her heart.
AEGISTHUS
And is it true, their story, that he is dead?
ELECTRA
It's truer than words: they brought him back.
AEGISTHUS
I must see the body, see it for myself.

ELECTRA
See it, if you must. It's there to see.

AEGISTHUS
At last you've said something that pleases me.

ELECTRA
Be pleased then, if it pleases you so much.

AEGISTHUS
Be quiet. Slaves, open the doors, and show
All the people what there is to see, inside.

The doors of the palace are opened. CLYTEMNESTRA*'s body, covered with a cloth, is revealed.* ORESTES *and* PYLADES, *swords drawn, stand beside it.*

People of Argos, look! The empty hopes
He gave you once are dead. Learn from this corpse
To bow to my yoke, to accept the bit.
Disobey, and you will suffer. Learn that now!

ELECTRA
My lesson is learned. I have understood,
At last, to accept what I cannot change.

AEGISTHUS
O Zeus, the hand of god was here: justice,
More than we can understand, is done.
Uncover the face. I am a relative,
And I must pay the dead my last respects.

ORESTES
Lift the cloth yourself. It is your duty,
Not mine, to view the corpse and say farewell.

AEGISTHUS
You're right. Slave, go inside: ask the queen to come.

ORESTES
There is no need to fetch her. She is here.

AEGISTHUS *lifts the cloth from the face of the corpse.*

AEGISTHUS
O gods! What sight is this?

ORESTES
Look, and see. Are you afraid?

AEGISTHUS
Who are you? Answer. What trap is this?
ORESTES
You called me dead; I am alive again.
AEGISTHUS
Orestes! God help me. Now I understand.
ORESTES
Priest-king! Prophet-king! At last you see!
AEGISTHUS
My death is near: there is no escape.
Before you kill me, let me say this –
ELECTRA
No, Orestes, no! Let him say nothing!
He's in the noose, the trap is sprung –
What good will it do
To allow him a little time? Kill him now,
At once – and throw his corpse
For dogs to maul, out of our sight.
He has brought us pain and misery:
Punish him! Kill him now, as he deserves!
ORESTES
Go inside, you, quickly. The answer now
Is not more words: it is your death.
AEGISTHUS
Why must we go inside? If what you're doing
Is right, why hide it? Murder me out here!
ORESTES
Give no more orders. Go inside.
Where you killed my father, there you must die.
AEGISTHUS
The palace of the children of Atreus!
Must it see death after death, for evermore?
ORESTES
It will see yours. That much, at least, is sure.
AEGISTHUS
And what of your own death, if you kill me?
I die for your father – you will die for me.
ORESTES
Still you invent arguments! Go inside.
It is time.

AEGISTHUS
Lead the way.
ORESTES
No: you must go first.
AEGISTHUS
In case I escape?
ORESTES
No. You must not know,
Or choose, the exact moment of your death.
You must suffer, and suffer to the end.
A sharp, sudden death: if that was the price
All criminals paid, there would soon be no more crime.
WOMEN (*as they go in*)
Children of Atreus, from great suffering
You have won freedom at last
By what has been done here, today.

Antigone

The legend

Before Oedipus was born, the gods foretold that he would murder his father and marry his own mother. His parents left him on a mountainside to die, but he was rescued and brought up in a foreign kingdom. When he was grown-up he went back by chance to his native land, and the prophecy was fulfilled. Without knowing who they were, he killed his father Laios, King of Thebes, and married his own mother Jocasta.

Four children were born to Oedipus and Jocasta: two sons, Eteocles and Polynices, and two daughters, Antigone and Ismene. They were still children when their father discovered the truth, blinded himself as a punishment, and went into exile. Creon, the queen's brother, acted as ruler of Thebes until the children grew up.

When Eteocles and Polynices reached manhood, they quarrelled about who should be king. Polynices went to collect an army from Thebes' Argive enemies, and came back to win the city for himself. Eteocles led an army of Theban champions.

The Thebans won. But during the battle the two brothers, Eteocles the patriot and Polynices the traitor, met in single combat, and each killed the other.

The play

Antigone continues the story from that point, beginning on the morning after the battle. Its subject is right and wrong. Firstly, what *men* think is right and wrong: how far we should go if we believe we are right, and when and how we should be prepared to give in to others. And secondly, what the *gods* call right and wrong, and the way men react to powers outside themselves.

Each of the characters takes a different viewpoint: not just Antigone and Creon, but also Ismene, the Soldier and Teiresias. The Chorus, too, makes an important commentary in the odes that separate the dialogue scenes.

Antigone is even more formally written than *Electra*, with balancing pairs of characters, debate-like arguments, and particularly symmetrical songs for the chorus. The characters are less roundly developed than in *Electra*, and this, together with the formal style, throws great weight on the religious problem at the heart of the play.

Antigone was first performed in 442 B.C.

Antigone

CHARACTERS

ANTIGONE
ISMENE
CREON, King of Thebes
SOLDIER
HAIMON, Creon's son
TEIRESIAS, the blind prophet
MESSENGER
EURYDICE, Queen of Thebes

GUARDS, SERVANTS

CHORUS OF OLD MEN

A courtyard outside the royal palace of Thebes. In the background, the palace doors.
Day.
ANTIGONE *is waiting anxiously.* ISMENE *comes in (by a smaller door in the main palace doors).*
ANTIGONE *hurries to her.*

ANTIGONE
O Ismene, Ismene my dear sister,
We are the last survivors, you and I,
Of the house of Oedipus – and still Zeus
Torments us with our father's crimes. What pain
Or suffering, what shame or dishonour
Have we not endured together? Now they say
That general Creon has proclaimed another law
In Thebes. Have they told you yet?
Have you heard the latest outrage, heard
How they are treating those we love as enemies?

ISMENE
Antigone, I've heard no news of those we love,
Good or bad, since our two dear brothers
Were snatched from us in a single blow,
Each killing the other. During the night
The enemy army has fled to Argos:
Since then no other news has reached me,
To gladden my heart or burden it with grief.

ANTIGONE
I knew it: that's why I sent for you out here,
Outside the palace, where no one will overhear.

ISMENE
What is it? What dark news is haunting you?

ANTIGONE
Our brothers' burial. Have you not heard
How Creon is honouring one, dishonouring the other?
They say he has buried Eteocles
Nobly, with all the pomp and ceremony
That will bring him honour with the dead below.
But the unhappy corpse of Polynices –
They say it's proclaimed to the whole of Thebes
That no one must bury him or weep for him;
He's to be left unmourned and unentombed,
A treasure-house of flesh for circling birds.
So says the worthy Creon – clear orders
For you and for me. Yes, for me! And now
He's coming here to proclaim it again,
Clearly, so that no one can claim ignorance.
It's no light matter: to disobey
Means death, by public stoning in the streets.
There. You know it all. Now you can show
If you remember, or forget, your royal birth.

ISMENE
My poor sister, if this is how things are,
What can I do or undo that will change them?

ANTIGONE
Think! Will you help me? Will you share the work?

ISMENE
What work, Antigone? What do you mean?

ANTIGONE
Will you come with me, and lift the corpse with me?

ISMENE
What, bury him? You mean, to break the law?

ANTIGONE
I mean to bury my brother – and yours too,
Whether you will or not. *I* shan't betray him!

ISMENE
How can you dare, when Creon has proclaimed – ?

ANTIGONE
He has no right to keep me from my own.
ISMENE
O Antigone, think! Think how our father died
Hated and miserable, tearing out his eyes
To pay for crimes he brought to light himself;
And think of her, his mother-wife,
Choking her life away in a twisted noose;
Think of our brothers, dead on a single day,
Unhappy victims of a common fate,
Each murdering the other.
Now we two are left, we two alone –
And think how we shall die, most miserable
Of all, if we defy the law, and break
The king's clear orders. No! We are women,
Antigone – not meant to fight with men.
We are the subjects of a powerful king,
And must obey in this and worse than this.
I pray to the dead below to pardon me:
I have no choice; I must obey the king.
ANTIGONE
If that's your choice, I accept it. Even if
You offered your help, I'd refuse it, now.
Your path is set. But I shall bury him –
And if I die for it, death will be sweet:
Convicted of reverence, I shall lie
Forever beside the brother who loves me,
The brother I love. I must please the dead
More than the living: for I'll lie in death
Forever. You've chosen to defy
The laws of heaven; the choice was yours to make.
ISMENE
I'm not defying the laws of heaven – but
I dare not break the laws the state lays down.
ANTIGONE
Make that your explanation. I shall go
And bury him, bury the brother I love.
ISMENE
Antigone, no! I'm afraid for you.
ANTIGONE
Don't be afraid for me. Look to yourself.

ISMENE
Bury him, then, if you have no other choice.
But hide it, tell no one. I'll keep silent too.

ANTIGONE
No! Cry it aloud! Proclaim it
To the whole of Thebes, or I'll despise you more!

ISMENE
Your heart is hot for such a chilling deed.

ANTIGONE
I know I'm pleasing those I have to please.

ISMENE
Yes, if you can – if only you have the strength.

ANTIGONE
If my strength fails, I'll stop – but not before.

ISMENE
It's madness to chase what you will never catch.

ANTIGONE
Don't call it madness, or you'll earn my hate,
And our dear dead brother will hate you too.
Leave me to my madness; leave me to do
What must be done, and bear what must be borne.
The most I'll suffer is a noble death.

ISMENE
Go on then, if you must. But remember,
Madness or not, your loved ones love you still!

She goes into the palace. ANTIGONE *goes out by one of the side doors.*
Music. The OLD MEN *come in. They speak sometimes separately, sometimes together. Their words are accompanied by music and choral movement.*

OLD MEN
O light of day,
The brightest that ever dawned
Over Thebes of the seven gates;
Eye of the golden morning
That glints at last
On the waters of Dirke,
You put to headlong flight
The champion of Argos,
Who came on our city in the pride

Of his white shield gleaming:
He came, and was driven back.

Polynices raised an army against us,
To fight a disputed claim;
Screaming defiance, he swooped
Like an eagle low across our land,
His white wings beating,
An army his talons,
His crest their helmet-plumes.

Like an eagle then
He hovered above us; he prowled
Round our city of seven gates,
His spears thirsty for blood.
But before he could gorge himself
On the heart's-blood of Thebes,
Before he could burn our crown of towers,
He was driven away;
The roar of battle rose around him
As he fought a dragon-adversary,
An enemy he could never beat.

For lord Zeus, who hates
The proud tongue's boasting, watched
His glittering army flood the plain,
Proud in their ringing gold;
Zeus watched, and hurled them down
In a thunderbolt, as they stood
Baying victory at the battlements.

Down to the ground he toppled,
Their torch-bearer who raged against us,
Urged on by savage madness,
A storm of hatred in his heart.
Down he fell; and Ares the war-god
Dealt each man a different death,
Ares our champion,
Yoked beside us in the fighting.

Seven champions at seven gates
Offered their enemies' armour up
To Zeus who rules the fight.

And those doomed brothers, sons
Of one father, one mother, raised
Spears against each other, died
In a single, common death.

So glorious victory smiled
On Thebes, city of chariots;
So now we celebrate,
Forgetting the cares of war.
Let us dance the night away
In the gods' temples, singing
To Bacchus our lord
To lead the dance in Thebes.

FIRST OLD MAN

But here comes the king,
Creon son of Menoiceus,
A new leader in a time
Of new prosperity. He has called
His counsellors together;
Summoned by royal decree,
We have gathered to hear him speak.

CREON *comes out of the palace, with his* SERVANTS. *He speaks formally: a king addressing his counsellors.*

CREON

Thebans, the gods have tossed our ship of state
In stormy waters, and set it on course again.
I sent my messengers to bring you here,
Chosen from all the people, because I remember
Your loyalty when Laios was King of Thebes,
Your loyalty to Oedipus his son, and then
To Eteocles and Polynices, his children.
You have been faithful to all the royal house;
And now that Oedipus' sons are dead – killed
On a single day, each by the other's hand,
Each one the victim, each the murderer –
The throne and power are mine, by right of blood.

There's no other way to test a man,
To learn the true temper of his heart and mind,

Than by seeing him practise the use of power.
My own opinion is that any king
Whose rule is absolute, who locks his lips
From fear, and refuses to seek advice, is doomed
And dangerous. And next to him, I hate
A man who sets his friends above the state.
I swear by Zeus above, who sees all things,
That if I see some danger threatening
The people, I shall denounce it; and no man
Who is their enemy will ever be my friend.
For Thebes, our ship of state, protects us all:
In her safe voyage lies all our hope of friends.

These are the policies by which I mean
To guard our city's greatness. And these rules
Lead me to make the following proclamation
Concerning the sons of Oedipus:
Eteocles died nobly, fighting for Thebes:
He is to be buried with all the pomp
And honour we owe the illustrious dead.
But his brother Polynices, a traitor
Who returned from exile to burn and sack
His country and its gods, to glut himself
On his own people's blood, and make them slaves –
He is to be left to rot, a feast for birds
And dogs, a mangled corpse for all to see.

Those are my orders: for no one will say
That I honoured evil men more than good.
Only a man loyal to Thebes
Can win my praise, alive or dead.

FIRST OLD MAN

My lord Creon, your will is clear,
Both for the hero and the traitor.
And your will is law, for those
Who died and those who live alike.

CREON

See, then, that no one disobeys.

FIRST OLD MAN

My lord, a younger man could guard –

CREON

There are guards on the corpse already.

FIRST OLD MAN
What else remains for us to do?
CREON
Let no one disobey the law.
FIRST OLD MAN
Only a fool would choose to die.
CREON
Death is the penalty. But men
Have often died in hope of gain.

A SOLDIER *comes in from one side, and kneels before* CREON.

SOLDIER
My lord, no one can say I'm out of breath
From hurrying, or that I came hot-foot
To bring you the news. I didn't want
To come; I kept stopping and thinking on the way.
'You fool,' I said to myself, 'why go at all?
You'll only suffer for it.' Then I thought,
'But what if Creon hears from someone else?
You'll suffer then, all right.' No easy job
Deciding – a short road soon became a long one.
But in the end I thought I'd better come
And tell you what I can – which isn't much.
If I suffer for it, I suffer – after all,
I can't be punished more than fate allows.
CREON
What's happened? Why are you so afraid to speak?
SOLDIER
Sir, let me tell you first, it wasn't me:
I didn't do it, and I didn't see
Who did. I'm innocent – I can't be blamed.
CREON
Another hedge of words! What is this news
That you're so reluctant to tell me?
SOLDIER
Bad news, my lord: that's why I'm scared to speak.
CREON
Bad news or not, just tell it me and go!
SOLDIER
All right, my lord. It's this. The corpse – someone

Has been and buried it. They sprinkled it
With a handful of dry dust: the usual rites.

CREON

Buried – the corpse? What man has dared – ?

SOLDIER

I don't know, my lord. The ground's hard and dry;
There were no signs that a pick or shovel
Had been used, no marks of wheels.
Whoever buried him left no tracks at all.
When the guard on the first watch showed us
What had happened, we were amazed:
The corpse was covered – not completely buried
With a proper funeral mound, just veiled
With a thin layer of dust, as if some passer-by
Had covered him up to ward off a curse.
There were no signs that dogs or wild beasts
Had been near: nothing had picked at his flesh.

We began shouting at each other right away,
Each man accusing the others of doing it.
It might have ended in a fight – and who
Was there to stop us? After all, any one
Of us could have buried him: no one could prove it,
One way or the other. We were all ready
To pick up red-hot iron, or walk through fire,
And swear by all the gods we hadn't done it
Or known of anyone planning it or doing it.

We searched for clues, but found nothing.
Then someone said something that shut us all up quick,
Made us hang our heads and shuffle our feet –
It meant trouble, whether we did as he said or not.
You had to be told, he said: we couldn't hide it.
Well, to cut it short, we drew lots, and I
Was the unlucky one. So here I am:
As unwilling to tell as you are to hear.
For no one likes a man who brings bad news.

FIRST OLD MAN

My lord, I wonder – is it possible
That what he's told us is the work of the gods?

CREON

Be quiet, old man, or I shall lose my temper.

You're old – don't prove yourself a fool as well.
I'll not have it said that the gods took thought
For that man's corpse. I suppose you think
They honoured him for loyal service,
Buried him nobly, this traitor who came
To burn their pillared temples, sack their shrines,
Destroy their land and scatter their laws?
I suppose you think they honour criminals?

No. The gods had no part in this. I know
There's a faction in the city who oppose me,
Who shake their heads in secret, rejecting
My royal authority, chafing against the yoke.
This is their doing! I know it: they'll have bribed
Others to bury him. Eagerness for money
Is the greatest curse of all. It breaks up homes,
Destroys cities, twists the minds of men,
Turns them from honesty and leads them on
To break their country's laws and despise the gods.

But this time their bribery will cost them dear.
Listen to me now, for I swear it by Zeus above:
Unless you find whoever buried him
And bring them here to me, you'll pay for it –
And not with death alone. You'll be tortured,
All of you, tormented till your guilt is clear,
And you learn in future where to go for gain.
The wages of sin are misery, not joy.

SOLDIER

Sir, may I speak? Or shall I turn and go?

CREON

You know that every word you say offends me.

SOLDIER

Offends your ears, my lord, or hurts your heart?

CREON

Offends me? Hurts me? What's that to you?

SOLDIER

The criminal hurts your heart; I hurt your ears.

CREON

Is there some point in all this arguing?

SOLDIER

The point is this, sir: I'm innocent.

CREON

You're guilty: you bartered your life for cash.

SOLDIER

My lord, you think
You've guessed the truth – but your guess is wrong.

CREON

Well, right or wrong, I tell you this; unless
You catch the criminals and bring them here
To me, those bribes you took will cost your life.

He goes into the palace. When he is out of hearing, the SOLDIER *shouts defiantly after him:*

SOLDIER

I hope they're caught, then! But I'll tell you this:
Catch them or not, whatever chance decides,
You won't catch *me* back here again. The gods
Saved me this time – but one chance is enough.

He goes out by the side-exit.

OLD MEN

There are many wonders,
But nothing more wonderful than man.
He travels the white sea
In the teeth of the storm,
Braving the roar and surge
Of the waters; he works
The oldest of the gods,
Immemorial, unbroken Earth:
His plough furrows her cheeks
As he follows the patient horses
And year succeeds to year.

Man is capable and cunning:
With snares and woven nets
He traps the birds of the air,
The creatures of the field
And the fish in the sea;
In the high hills he takes
The wild beasts of the mountains;
He tames proud horses,
Their wild manes flying,

And breaks mighty mountain bulls
Till they learn to bear his yoke.

He has learned speech
And wind-swift thought,
The manners of cities
And the laws of living together;
He knows how to escape the frost
That comes from a clear sky,
And the arrows of the rain;
He has ample skill, to match
Whatever the future brings –
For every disease a cure
But Death, which has no cure.

With wisdom and fertile skill,
Cunning past fancy's dream,
He can choose to follow good
Or evil. When he keeps the laws
Of the land, the sacred laws
Of heaven, his city stands high:
Cityless only are those
Who turn to evil in their rashness;
We must forbid them
Our hearths and homes,
Forbid them our thoughts themselves.

FIRST OLD MAN
O gods!
What sight is this?
Surely we know her?
Antigone!
Unhappy daughter of unhappy Oedipus,
Was it you so rash
As to break King Creon's law?

The SOLDIER *comes in, with* GUARDS *bringing* ANTIGONE.

SOLDIER
Here she is! Here's the one who did it. We caught
Her red-handed, burying him. Where's King Creon?

FIRST OLD MAN
Here: coming out of the palace just in time.

CREON *comes out of the palace, alone.*

CREON
Coming out in time for what? What's happened now?
SOLDIER
My lord, it's a mistake to swear oaths and promises:
You may have to change your mind. The last time
I was here, and shivering at your threats, I swore
That nothing on earth would bring me back again.
But I was wrong: a piece of luck has come,
So unexpected that it's brought me back,
Broken oaths or not. I've brought you this girl:
We caught her burying the corpse. No need
To cast lots this time, who was to come: the luck
Was mine and no one else's. Here she is:
Take her and question her any way you please.
I'm free of it – my innocence is proved.
CREON
What was she doing when you arrested her?
SOLDIER
She was burying the body. Just that, no more.
CREON
You're sure? You realise what you're saying?
SOLDIER
I'm saying I saw her burying the corpse
You said no one must touch. Is that not plain?
CREON
Tell me in detail, everything that happened.
SOLDIER
It was like this. When we got back, our ears
Still stinging with your threats, we swept the dust
Clear of the body, and left it
Naked and sodden on the plain. Then we took
Our position on a little hill, upwind
Of him to escape the stink. This time we kept
A careful watch, cursing each other to keep
Ourselves alert. That's how it was till noon,
When the sun was right overhead, and the heat
Was really blazing down. Then, suddenly,
Out of nowhere, a huge wind blew up
And filled the sky, flattening the leaves

And covering the plain. The air was full
Of dust: it was a plague sent by the gods,
And we screwed our eyes tight shut till it was done.

After a long time, it blew over – and then
We saw the girl, crying a bitter cry,
Like a mother bird come home to find her nestlings gone.
She stood there weeping by the naked corpse,
Weeping and cursing whoever had swept him clean.
But then she brought handfuls of dry dust,
And lifted up a fine bronze jug she had,
To pour the offerings we pay the dead.
As soon as we saw that we hurried down
And arrested her. She wasn't afraid; and when
We charged her with this and the other burial,
She didn't deny it. I was glad of that,
And sorry too. Glad to be safe myself,
Sorry for her sake, who'd never done me harm.
Still, sorry or not, my innocence is proved:
I've saved my own skin, and that's what matters most.

CREON

Antigone . . . Antigone, look at me . . .
Do you admit this crime, or deny it?

ANTIGONE

Yes, I admit it. There's nothing to deny.

CREON (*to the* SOLDIER)

In that case, you may go. You're free from blame.
Now, Antigone, tell me, yes or no,
Did you know of my order forbidding this?

ANTIGONE

After your proclamation, all Thebes knew.

CREON

You knew – and still you dared to disobey?

ANTIGONE

Yes. For it was not Zeus who made this law,
Or Justice, who dwells with the gods below –
It was you, a mortal. And I thought
No mortal's proclamation strong enough
To over-rule the gods' unwritten laws,
Laws not made to last for a day or a year,
But forever, unfailing and eternal,

Laws no mortal man could ever make me break,
And answer for it to the gods. The penalty
Was death – I knew that. But I also knew,
Without needing your proclamation to tell me,
That I would have to die one day, soon or late.
And can you not see how I long for death?
My life is a sea of pain: when death comes
I shall bear it easily. What I could not bear
Would be the thought that I'd left my brother,
My own mother's son, to rot unburied –
That would have been unbearable, not this.
Does that seem foolish to you? If so,
Consider this: which is more foolish, my love
For my brother, or your law calling it a crime?

FIRST OLD MAN

She's proud and stubborn, her father's daughter.
She has never learned to give way to troubles.

CREON

She'll give way! Great pride brings a greater fall.
The hardest iron, baked in the hottest fire,
Is first to snap; a little bridle tames
The proudest horse; Antigone will give way.
A slave has no room for pride – as she is proud,
Proud when she broke the law I had proclaimed,
Proud now, exulting in what she has done,
Laughing at Justice. Am I the King of Thebes
Or is she? No, my lord: I'll punish her
As I proclaimed I would. She's my niece,
But even if she was nearest to me in blood
Of all who worship Zeus at the family altar,
She and her sister would not escape their fate.
Her sister, yes! She had a hand in this:
She shared this burial. Bring her out here!
I saw her just now inside the palace,
Weeping, distracted by grief. So criminals
Often betray crimes plotted in the dark,
Before they can commit them. Only this
Is worse: to be caught, and glory in the crime.

ANTIGONE

The penalty was death. Is that enough?

CREON
I shall be satisfied with your death, yes.
ANTIGONE
Why delay, then? Why not kill me now?
We have no more to say to one another.
I have buried my brother, and won, by that,
The greatest glory I could have wished for.
I know that everyone in Thebes agrees –
Only fear of you prevents them speaking out.
Of all the blessings tyrants have, the best
Is doing and saying exactly as they please.
CREON
No! You're alone! No one in Thebes agrees.
ANTIGONE
They do – but they fear you, and say nothing.
CREON
I tell you you're alone. Are you not ashamed?
ANTIGONE
Ashamed? Ashamed of loving my own brother?
CREON
And was his enemy not your brother too?
ANTIGONE
Yes. Eteocles was my brother too.
CREON
And don't you see how you dishonour him?
ANTIGONE
My dear dead brother knows I honour him.
CREON
What honour? The honour you give a criminal?
ANTIGONE
It was his brother, not a slave, who died.
CREON
Yes: died attacking Thebes, while he defended it.
ANTIGONE
Now they're dead, we owe them equal honour.
CREON
Equal honour? A traitor and a hero?
ANTIGONE
Their death is the same, and makes them equal.
CREON
An enemy cannot be loved, even in death.

ANTIGONE
I was born to love, not hate, my brothers.

CREON
Love them, then! Go to Hades, and love them there!
No woman will rule in Thebes while I am king!

GUARDS *bring in* ISMENE *from the palace.*

FIRST OLD MAN
Here comes Ismene from the palace,
Weeping a sister's tears:
A dark cloud of grief
Darkens her forehead,
Overshadows her beauty
And dews her cheeks with tears.

CREON
Come here, you viper! Lurking in my house,
You and your sister, like twin fiends from hell
That feed in secret on my blood, and plan
To destroy my power! Come here, and answer me:
Did you share in this burial, yes or no?

ISMENE
I shared in it, if only she agrees!
I shared in it, and I must share the blame.

ANTIGONE
No! Justice will not allow it. You refused
To help me; I gave you no part in it.

ISMENE
But now you are sailing a stormy sea;
Let me stand beside you, and share your suffering.

ANTIGONE
Death and the dead are witnesses who did
The deed. You can't love with words alone.

ISMENE
O Antigone, let me die with you
And share with you in honouring the dead!

ANTIGONE
You took no part before; you have no claim
To take part now. My death will be enough.

ISMENE
What life is left for me, when you are dead?

ANTIGONE
Ask Creon: isn't he the one you love?
ISMENE
How can you help yourself by mocking me?
ANTIGONE
This is grim mockery, that brings no joy.
ISMENE
O sister, what can I do to help you now?
ANTIGONE
Save yourself. I won't begrudge you that.
ISMENE
Please let me share your fate, and die with you!
ANTIGONE
You chose to live; it was I who chose to die.
ISMENE
I warned you then, that it would end in death.
ANTIGONE
Your actions pleased the living, mine the dead.
ISMENE
Then each of us is guilty! Each is wrong!
ANTIGONE
Be comforted. You have your life; I gave
Mine long ago, in service to the dead.
CREON
The pair of them are mad! One mad from birth,
The other showing her madness only now.
ISMENE
Just so, my lord: the wits we have from birth
Are soon destroyed by miseries like these.
CREON
As yours were, when you chose to share her guilt!
ISMENE
What life is left for me, when she is dead?
CREON
Count her as dead already: her life is over.
ISMENE
But my lord – will you kill your own son's bride?
CREON
There will be other fields for him to plough.
ISMENE
No greater love was ever seen than theirs.

CREON
My son was not born to marry criminals.

ANTIGONE
O Haimon, dearest, how your father mocks you!

CREON
Enough of your marriage – and enough of you!

FIRST OLD MAN
My lord, will you part your own son from his bride?

CREON
Her death will part them; I am not to blame.

FIRST OLD MAN
It's decided, then? She must die?

CREON
Decided, yes – for you and for me. Guards!
Take them inside at once, and let them learn
The proper place of women: no more roaming
Outside the palace walls. Even brave men
Attempt escape, when death's approach is near.

GUARDS *take* ANTIGONE *and* ISMENE *into the palace.* CREON *remains onstage.*

OLD MEN
Happy are those whose lives are free
Of the taste of disaster:
For when a house is shaken by the gods
It lies cursed forever,
Generation to generation.
It is like the waves of the swollen sea,
Driven by winds from Thrace
Across the dark face of the waters,
Stirring black sand from the depths
As they hurl themselves on
To roar and crash on stubborn cliffs
Fronting the teeth of the storm.

The house of Labdacus is cursed,
The sorrows of the living heaped
On the sorrows of the dead. Generation
To generation, god punishes them:
There can be no escape.
The hope of the house flickered

In the last roots of the children
Of Oedipus, flickered and was gone,
Quenched by a layer of blood-stained dust
Offered to the gods of death,
Quenched by madness of speech
And frenzy in the heart.

O Zeus, what arrogance of man
Can ever check your power?
Even Sleep, who snares all things,
Is powerless against it;
The unwearying months of the gods
Cannot master it;
Old age cannot make it grey.
You are and always shall be
Lord of the dazzling halls
Of marble Olympus.
In the past and the future,
Near and far, this law
Is fixed and unchanging forever:
When greatness enters mortal life
It brings disaster, always.

Hope wanders the wide world,
Comforting many men;
But this same fond hope
Lures others to disaster
In the foolish longings of their hearts:
Innocent and ignorant
They blunder on
Till their feet are in the fire.
It was wisely said
That evil always seems good
To those whose minds the gods
Are drawing towards disaster:
Only for the briefest moment
Can they find a breathing-space
Untainted with disaster.

HAIMON *comes in from the palace.*

FIRST OLD MAN
Here is Haimon, my lord,

Your last surviving son.
Has he come to grieve
For Antigone, his promised bride?
Is there bitterness in his heart
For the hope of his marriage lost?

CREON

We'll soon know, and need no seer to tell us.
Haimon, my son, have you come to rage at me
For condemning your bride? Or do you still
Respect and honour me, in spite of it?

HAIMON

Father, I am your son. Your wisdom rules
My life, and I shall always respect it.
How could a marriage matter more to me
Than walking always in the path you choose?

CREON

A wise choice, my son, to keep your father's will
Always before you, and follow it in your heart.
This is what all men pray for: loyal sons
Who grow in duty and obedience,
Who fight their fathers' enemies
And honour their fathers' friends. A man
Whose sons are rebellious and discontented
Breeds nothing but trouble for himself
And laughter for his enemies. Don't let
Lust for a woman drive out your common sense.
A worthless wife, a criminal, will bring
Your bed cold comfort; nothing bites so deep
As treachery from those we love. Forget
Her, then! Call her an enemy, and let
Her find herself a husband in Hades.
Antigone! Convicted of disobedience,
The only traitor in the whole of Thebes.
I'll not make myself a traitor too:
I'll kill her as I proclaimed I would.
My own niece! Well may she cry to Zeus
Lord of Kinship – if I allowed my own kin
To disobey, how could I punish strangers?
Justice at home breeds justice in the state.

I trust a man who keeps the law: he'll make
An honest subject or an honest king,

A loyal companion on the battlefield,
A friend, trusted and true. But those who break
The law, who set themselves above the king,
I hold beneath contempt. We must obey
The man the city chooses, in all things,
Just or unjust, great or small. For there is
No greater evil than disobedience:
Great cities are devoured by it, their homes
Left empty, their armies scattered and destroyed.
In a prosperous state, where all is well,
Obedience is the cause. That's why
I mean to uphold the law, and not give way,
Defeated by a woman. I'd yield,
If need be, to a man: but no one will say
A woman defeated Creon, king of Thebes.

FIRST OLD MAN

My lord, I think – unless I'm deceived
By age – that all you say is common sense.

HAIMON

Father, the gods above send us wisdom,
The most precious gift of all.
How can I argue with you? It would take
A wiser man than me to prove you wrong.
But there are others who think differently:
I am your eyes and ears in Thebes; I know
What each man says and does, praises or blames.
The king's frown silences a man,
Makes him say only what he thinks will please;
But I hear them murmur in the shadows –
I hear their secret thoughts. And they're full
Of pity for Antigone. They say
Her punishment is cruel and undeserved:
She buried her own brother, dead in battle,
Instead of leaving his corpse for dogs and birds
To pick. She's earned a golden crown, not death –
Such is the secret talk I hear in Thebes.

Father, nothing else matters more to me
Than your good name. What greater prize
Could any son – or any father – ask?
And for the sake of that good name, I ask you

To give way now, admit you were wrong, and change
Your mind. Only fools think that they alone
Are wise, and hear no other point of view.
A wise man is never ashamed to learn,
To listen, and bend when the time is right.
When a flood sweeps through a forest, the trees
That bend survive, keep every leaf intact;
The ones that don't snap off and are swept away.
A wise man knows when to slacken sail;
A fool refuses and overturns his ship.
Give up your anger, father: change your mind!
Accept my advice, young as I am;
No man is born infallible, however much
We might prefer it – and the next best thing
Is to be willing to follow wise advice.

FIRST OLD MAN
My lord, he's spoken well, as you did.
If his advice is good, you should take heed.

CREON
Take heed of him? I'm a grown man, my lord –
Am I to take lessons from a boy his age?

HAIMON
Of course, if what I say is right! It's not
My age that matters – it's knowing right from wrong!

CREON
And it's right to honour those who break the law?

HAIMON
Not if that means honouring criminals.

CREON
And Antigone – isn't she a criminal?

HAIMON
No one in Thebes calls what she did a crime.

CREON
No one in Thebes? I don't take orders from Thebes.

HAIMON
Now you're the one who's talking like a boy.

CREON
I'm the king: I rule by my own authority.

HAIMON
No city belongs to any single man.

CREON
The city is the king's – that is the law.

HAIMON
Yes – if you rule a desert state, alone.

CREON (*to the* OLD MEN)
You see? He's fighting on the woman's side.

HAIMON
Only if you're the woman! I'm fighting for you.

CREON
For me? When every word defies me?

HAIMON
I defy you only when I see you're wrong.

CREON
How is it wrong to defend my own royal power?

HAIMON
A fine defence, when you defy the gods!

CREON
What is there worse than being a woman's slave?

HAIMON
To be the slave of evil – that is worse.

CREON
Every word you say is for Antigone!

HAIMON
And for you, and me, and the gods below.

CREON
I tell you you'll never marry her alive.

HAIMON
And I tell you she won't be the only one to die.

CREON
Is that a threat? Are you so insolent – ?

HAIMON
Is it insolence to argue with a fool?

CREON
A fool teaches me wisdom – to his cost!

HAIMON
Father, you're talking like a madman.

CREON
Father? Don't 'father' me, you woman's slave!

HAIMON
You refuse to listen? You won't allow –

CREON
I've allowed too much already. Gods above!
You'll regret this insolence. Guards! Bring her out
And kill her here! Let her bridegroom watch her die!

HAIMON
No! That I'll never see! And from this hour
You'll never see my face again. Let others stay
And watch you play the madman – I have done!

He hurries out.

FIRST OLD MAN
He's gone, my lord, blazing with anger.
A boy's anger – who knows where it will end?

CREON
Let it end where it likes! Let him think as he likes!
The pair of them are doomed: he can't save them now.

FIRST OLD MAN
You mean to kill both sisters, then, my lord?

CREON
No: you're right. Ismene is innocent.

FIRST OLD MAN
And the other one? What way is she to die?

CREON
The guards will take her to a desert place
And wall her up in living rock, with food
Enough to free our city from the taint
Of murder. There she can sing her hymns to Death,
Lord of the underworld, the only god
She honours – sing to him to spare her life.
For she must learn at last that it is pain
And wasted labour to worship Death alone.

He goes.

OLD MEN
Love cannot be conquered in battle
Or bought and sold for cash.
He is everywhere: encamped
On a girl's soft cheeks,
Riding the barren sea,
Peopling the wilderness.

When he shoots arrows of desire
No god, no man can escape
His madness.

Love twists even a just man's mind
And turns it to evil and shame.
He stirred this present strife,
Son against father.
His arrows glitter in the glance
Of a fair bride's eyes;
He sits enthroned in power.
When his goddess, Aphrodite, plays,
She wins with ease.

Music. GUARDS *lead* ANTIGONE *out in procession.*

FIRST OLD MAN
How shall we bear it? A cruel sight
To carry us beyond the bounds
Of loyalty, wells of tears unchecked:
They are leading Antigone
To the grave, and her marriage
With Death, who puts all men to sleep.

ANTIGONE
Citizens of Thebes,
I shall make no more journeys now;
Today I shall look my last
On the sun's bright light above.
For Death, who puts all men to sleep,
Is leading me, alive,
To the shores of the river of death.
There are no marriage-songs to sing,
No bridal hymns:
My marriage is with Death,
Lord of the world below.

FIRST OLD MAN
All praise and honour are yours
As you journey to the world below.
No sickness ravaged you,
No sword cut short your life;
Mistress of your own fate,
You chose this path yourself,

And now, alive, you go
Where no living man has gone before.

ANTIGONE

I have heard that once, in Phrygia,
Niobe, daughter of Tantalos,
Was entombed on the rocky heights
Of Sipylos. Like ivy clinging,
The creeping stone enfolded her,
And now, they say,
Unfailing rain, unfailing snow,
Falling like tears from her weeping eyes,
Bedews her breast. Like her, now,
The gods put me to rest.[6]

FIRST OLD MAN

And yet she was a goddess,
The child of immortal gods.
We are mortals, born of men.
Surely it is great honour
For a mortal to live
And die and be honoured in death
As was an immortal once.

ANTIGONE

This is mockery, my lord!
In the name of the gods of Thebes,
Save your laughter
Till I am gone forever.
O my lords,
O Thebes my city,
Washed by the streams of Dirke,
Thebes, city of chariots –
Remember the law I broke,
Remember my punishment.
I go to a strange new death
In a cave of living rock,
Alone, without a friend to grieve.
I have no kinship now
With those above the earth,
And none with the dead below.

FIRST OLD MAN

My child, you went
To the limits of daring,

And stumbled against the high throne
Of Justice. Perhaps this punishment
Is payment still
For the sins of Oedipus your father.

ANTIGONE

My lord, you have touched
On the deepest pain of all:
The bitter grief
Of Oedipus my father, the doom
On all of us,
The famous house of Labdacus.
That marriage-bed –
Mother coupling with son,
My own engendering!
My parents! And now I go
To them accursed, unwed.
And Polynices, too, made a marriage
That was doomed, and destroyed him –
O my brother, in death
You destroyed me too,
Destroyed your sister too.

FIRST OLD MAN

There is respect
For those who show respect;
But a great king in his power
Will not be challenged – it was
Your own stubbornness, your own fury,
That brought destruction down on you.

ANTIGONE

So now I begin my journey,
My last journey: alone, unwept,
Unmarried and most miserable.
It is the will of the gods
That I see the blessed sun
No more, that I go to my death
With no friend's tears to comfort me.

CREON *comes in angrily.*

CREON

If weeping and wailing at the gates of hell
Could buy death off, they'd never end.

Guards! Take her away at once,
And wall her up in a rocky cave alone
As I commanded you. There she can die,
Or live, if she prefers, in a stony tomb
Forever. No one can charge us with her death –
But she'll never see a living man again.

ANTIGONE

My hour has come. I must go to my tomb,
My rocky prison-cell, my marriage-bower.
I know I shall find them there, my dear ones,
Gathered in the congregation of the dead
By Queen Persephone. I am the last
To join them, last and most unhappy, snatched
Before my life is done. And will you smile
To greet me, there in the halls of death –
My father Oedipus, my unhappy mother,
And the brother I loved above life itself?
I honoured you all in death; I washed you
And laid you out; I poured libations
Beside your graves. It was for this
Last service to Polynices my brother
That I am thus rewarded – a service
Of honour that all right-thinking men approve.

If I had lost a husband or a son
And the city had stood against their burying,
I should have let them rot: another man
Could have married me, another son been born.
But where should I find another brother,
When my father and mother lie cold in death?
I honoured Polynices above the law –
And Creon condemns me, calls me a criminal,
And has me dragged to my death by force.

There is no one to sing my bridal-hymn;
I shall never have children to cherish;
I'm friendless and alone, accursed of fate
And condemned to a living death. What law,
What justice of the gods have I transgressed?
Why should we honour them or ask for their help,
If obedience to their laws is called a crime?
If that is so, and what has happened here

Is by their will, my death will prove it so.
But if the guilt is Creon's, may he learn
The truth in suffering as great as mine!

FIRST OLD MAN

The same storm-winds of madness
Are raging in her heart.

CREON

The guards are slow to lead
Her away. They'll suffer for it.

FIRST OLD MAN

Your words tremble
On the very brink of death.

CREON

There's no comfort I can offer:
The sentence must be carried out.

ANTIGONE

O city of Thebes,
Gods of my native land,
My hour is now!
Look down on me,
Princes of Thebes:
The last true daughter
Of your own royal house.
Look at my punishment
And those who punish me,
Rewarding piety with death.

The GUARDS *lead her out by the side-exit.*

OLD MEN

So beautiful Danaë exchanged
The light of day for the bronze walls
Of a prison cell: she was hidden away,
Kept close in a bridal bower
As secret as any grave.
She was a princess too,
My child, and kept
The seed of Zeus
That fell in the golden rain.
The power of fate is fearful:
Not wealth or war
Or city towers

Or dark ships beaten by the waves
Can stand against it.

So impetuous Lycurgus,
Son of Dryas, king of the Edonians,
Was imprisoned and bound
In a rocky prison cell,
To pay for his insolence to Dionysos.
There the cancer-growth
Of madness faded
Slowly from his mind; he learned
To love the god he once had mocked
In the frenzy of his heart.
He had tried to check the women,
Put out the Bacchic fire,
And he had angered the Muses
Who love to hear the flute.

By the dark rocks beside the double sea
Are the cliffs of Bosporos, and Salmydessos
In Thrace, where Ares the war-god,
Protector of the city, saw the accursed wound
Of blindness dealt her sons by a step-mother
Fierce in her anger: darkness dealt
On eyes that cried aloud for vengeance,
The shuttle stabbing like a dagger,
The step-mother's hands red with blood.

They wept sad tears then, storms of grief,
Sons of a mother cursed in her marriage.
She was a princess too, descended
From the ancient line of Erectheus;
She was the North Wind's child,
Nursed in a distant cave by the storm-winds
Swift as wild horses galloping in the hills.
She was descended from the gods, my child,
And still the aged Fates pressed her hard.[7]

TEIRESIAS *comes in, leaning on a blind man's stick, and led by a young* SERVANT.

TEIRESIAS

Princes of Thebes, we have come, the seer

And the boy, one pair of eyes to lead us both.
The blind must have a guide to show the way.

CREON

My lord Teiresias, what brings you here?

TEIRESIAS

Listen and obey: I speak Apollo's words.

CREON

Have I not always followed your advice?

TEIRESIAS

You have – to the great benefit of Thebes.

CREON

I am happy to acknowledge your wisdom.

TEIRESIAS

Then heed it now: for you stand on a razor's edge.

CREON

A dark saying, my lord. What does it mean?

TEIRESIAS

Listen to the omens the gods have sent.
I was in my ancient prophetic seat,
Where the birds gather to give me omens,
When all at once I heard their voices –
A strange, maddened screaming, as they tore
Each other with their talons, beating their wings
In a message not hard to understand.
I was alarmed, and went to sacrifice.
The fire was laid ready on the altar,
But when I tried to light it, it would not burn –
Instead, a hideous liquid mess oozed out
Over the ashes, hissing and spluttering;
The gall-bladder burst, and the fat melted
And dripped from the naked thighs. All this
I learned from the boy, who gives me eyes
So that I can see for others. The sacrifice
Had failed: the omens would tell me nothing.

There's a plague in Thebes, and its cause
Is you, my lord. Our oracles, our holy shrines
Have been polluted by dogs and birds
Gorged on the flesh of Polynices
Son of Oedipus; the gods refuse to hear us;
The altar-fires reject our sacrifice;

The birds of the air, drunk on human blood,
Have no clear oracles to send us. Think hard,
My son. It is common to all mankind
To make mistakes; but a prudent man
Admits his error, and tries to undo the wrong
He did. Only fools persist in stubbornness.
Give way: yield to the dead. Where is the sense
In killing a corpse twice over? Listen to me:
My advice is good, and you'd be wise to follow it.

CREON

I see you're just like the rest, old man,
An archer who makes the king his target.
So they've bribed a prophet against me now –
I'm their merchandise, to buy and sell
For gain! Well, I tell you this, my lord:
Not all your trafficking in wealth, not all
The gold in Sardis and in India will buy
Him burial; not even if Zeus' eagles
Carried him up to pollute their master's throne
Would I bury him to escape the curse.
For how can a mortal man pollute the gods?
It is a shameful thing, Teiresias
Lord of all wisdom, when a wise man sells
His wisdom, and utters lies to earn a fee!

TEIRESIAS

Alas! What man can truly say he knows – ?

CREON

What hackneyed proverb are you quoting now?

TEIRESIAS

I say that wisdom is man's richest gift.

CREON

Just so: and folly's his greatest curse.

TEIRESIAS

A curse you suffer from yourself, my lord.

CREON

I don't intend to argue with a priest.

TEIRESIAS

And yet you say my prophecies are lies.

CREON

I say that priests love money. That's all.

TEIRESIAS
And every tyrant loves to use his power.

CREON
You realise you are talking to your king?

TEIRESIAS
King of the land I saved for him: I do.

CREON
No one disputes your wisdom – or your greed.

TEIRESIAS
Be careful! There are dark secrets still to tell.

CREON
Well, tell them! But expect no gain from me.

TEIRESIAS
There's no gain for you in what I know.

CREON
My royal will is not for you to buy and sell.

TEIRESIAS
Then I'll tell you this. You will not live
Through many more circuits of the wheeling sun
Before you've given a son of your own loins
To death, in payment for your guilt:
First, for sending a child of the world above
To a rocky grave; and next, for keeping
Unburied, unhonoured, unsanctified, the corpse
That belongs not to you or the gods above
But to the dead below. For this crime,
This violence done to them, the gods of Hades
Have sent avenging Furies to punish you;
They're lying in wait, and they'll destroy you.

Is this the prophecy of one who lies
For money? Not many hours from now
Your palace will be filled with the desperate grief
Of men and women, and a storm of hate
Will be stirred against you in every city
Whose mangled sons have been buried in death
By dogs or beasts or the wheeling birds above,
Who have carried the unholy stench of death
Home to their household gods.

You challenged me,
And I have fired my arrows at your heart,

Arrows of grief whose wounds you will not escape.
Boy, take me home. Some younger man can stay
And face his fury, watch him check his tongue
And learn more wisdom than he has shown today.

He goes out, led by the BOY. CREON *stands as if thunderstruck.*

FIRST OLD MAN
My lord, he's gone, but his prophecies
Remain. Dreadful prophecies! In all the years
Since I who am old was a boy in Thebes
His prophecies have never once proved false.

CREON
It's true: I acknowledge it. And now
Whichever path I choose is fearful – to yield,
Or to stand firm and cause my own destruction.

FIRST OLD MAN
If I may give you good advice, my lord –

CREON
What must I do? Tell me: I'll obey.

FIRST OLD MAN
Go first and free the girl from her prison;
Then place the unburied body in a grave.

CREON
That's your advice? I must give way?

FIRST OLD MAN
As soon as you can, my lord. The gods are quick
To send disaster on mortals who disobey.

CREON
The decision is hard, but I accept it.
No man can fight Necessity and win.

FIRST OLD MAN
Go now yourself and do it. Trust no one else.

CREON
I shall, at once. Slaves! Come here! Quickly!
Bring spades and axes – hurry! – to the plain.
My decision is made: I imprisoned her
And I must set her free myself. I know
That the laws of the gods are fixed forever,
And man's duty is to obey them, always.

He hurries out.

OLD MEN
Lord Dionysos, god of many names,
Delight of your mother, Kadmus' daughter,
Son of almighty Zeus
Lord of the thunderbolt;
You are the guardian of Italy;
You rule the sheltered plains
Of Eleusis, where all are welcome
In the sacred mysteries;
You are Bacchus, lord of Thebes
The Bacchants' motherland,
By the waters of Ismenus
Where the savage dragon's teeth were sown.

You are seen where the torches gleam
On the twin peaks of Mount Parnassus,
Home of the mountain-nymphs,
Your Bacchant followers
In the sacred cave, secret
Beside the Castalian Spring.
You are sent to us from the ivied slopes
Of the hillsides of Nysa,
Shores green with clustering vines;
Your name is sung aloud
In more than mortal song
Through all the countryside of Thebes.

Thebes is the land you honour
Above all other lands,
Honour with your mother
Who died in the thunderblast.
Thebes, your land, lies sick,
Gripped hard by a fearful plague –
Come down and heal us, lord,
Step lightly across the heights of Parnassus
And the sighing waters of the sea.

The stars whose breath is fire
Follow your dancing steps;
You lead the singing
In the voices of the night;

Dionysus, son of Zeus,
With your attendants beside you,
Your worshippers in frenzy
Dancing the night away – Iacchus, lord,
Come down to us, and bless our land once more!

As they finish, the MESSENGER *comes in from the side-entrance.*

MESSENGER
Neighbours of Kadmus and of Amphion,
My lords of Thebes, I say that human life
Is a thing infirm and insubstantial,
Subject to fortune's whim. Chance lifts us up
And casts us down, rich man and beggar,
Ruler and ruled alike. No one can look
At our present circumstance, and tell the future.
Until today, King Creon was a man
I envied. He saved us from our enemies;
He held the sovereign power, and ruled us well,
A noble father blessed with noble sons.
Now all he had is gone. For when a man
Forfeits the joys of life, by his own fault,
He chooses a living death. Fill all your house
With riches, live in kingly state – if joy
Is absent, all you have is a wisp of smoke,
The shadow of a dream of happiness.

FIRST OLD MAN
What's happened? What grief for the royal house?

MESSENGER
They're dead, and the living caused their death.

FIRST OLD MAN
Dead? Who is dead? And who is the murderer? Speak.

MESSENGER
Haimon is dead. Killed by his own –

FIRST OLD MAN
His father?

MESSENGER
His own hand.
His fury at his father caused his death.

FIRST OLD MAN
Exactly as Teiresias foretold.

MESSENGER
And now, my lords, the future lies with you.

FIRST OLD MAN
Here comes the queen, unhappy Eurydice,
Creon's wife. Has she heard of Haimon's death,
Or has some other reason brought her here?

Queen EURYDICE *comes from the palace.*

EURYDICE
People of Thebes, I was on my way to offer
Prayers at the shrine of Pallas Athene;
My hand was on the latch, to open the door,
When I overheard news of some disaster,
New grief for the royal house. I fell back
In fear, into the arms of my maid-servants.
What has happened? Tell me the news again:
I have borne grief before, and I can bear it.

MESSENGER
My lady, I was present and saw it all;
I'll tell you exactly what happened.
What point in softening the blow,
And being proved a liar afterwards? The truth
Is always best.

I went with the king your husband
To the place far out on the edge of the plain
Where Polynices' body lay, torn by dogs,
A cruel sight. We washed what was left of him
In holy water, and prayed to Hecate,
Goddess of journeys, and Pluto, king
Of the underworld, to receive him with favour.
Then, on a pyre of fresh-cut branches, we burned
The remains, and buried his ashes
With reverence in a mound of his native earth.

When that was done, we hurried on towards
Antigone's rocky cell, where she was left
To make her unholy marriage with death.
We were still out of hearing, when they told
The king of hopeless, helpless weeping
From inside the tomb; and as he came nearer
The sound of bitter lamenting filled his ears,

And he groaned aloud and cried, 'Has what I feared
Come true? Is this the saddest journey
I must ever make? Is the crying I hear my son's?
Go quickly, some of you – there, where the stones
Have been dragged away. Go down into the tomb
And see if it is really Haimon's voice
I hear, or if the gods are mocking me.'

We went and looked, as our distracted master
Ordered. And there, in a corner of the cave,
We saw the girl hanging in a slender noose
Made from the woven linen of her dress.
The boy was kneeling beside her, his arms
Enfolding her waist. He was weeping bitterly
For his bride snatched from him to the dead below,
His father's crime, his own unhappy love.
When the king saw him, he groaned in anguish
And ran to him crying, 'Haimon, my child,
What have you done? What madness brought you here
To your own destruction? Come out of the cave; 1221
Come out, I beg you on my knees!'

The boy
Said nothing, looked at him with blazing eyes.
Then all at once he spat, full in his face,
And drew his sword. The father fled – and then,
Maddened with fury, the unhappy boy
Leaned his whole weight against the sword,
And pressed the blade home, deep in his own ribs.
With his last strength, he embraced the girl again;
His dying kisses sent a spurt of blood
To blush her pale cheeks red. And now they lie
Together, corpse with corpse, married at last
In death – a proof to all living men
That only disaster comes of stubbornness.

In the silence that follows, EURYDICE *goes inside.*

FIRST OLD MAN
What does it mean? The queen has turned
And gone inside without a word.

MESSENGER
Perhaps she is mindful of the custom,

And will not show her grief out here
In public, but has gone inside
To weep for her son in private.

FIRST OLD MAN

I hope so. But dumb grief like this
Is as ominous as a wild lament.

MESSENGER

I'll go inside and see, in case
Her sorrow prompts some desperate act.
Such silent grief is ominous.

He goes into the palace.

FIRST OLD MAN

Here comes the king,
Bearing in his arms
A burden that clearly tells
The destruction he brought
Down on himself, the work
Of no stranger's hands.

Music. CREON *enters, carrying* HAIMON*'s corpse in his arms.* GUARDS *follow with the body of* ANTIGONE.

CREON

Weep now for the sin committed,
Darkness in the soul
Stubborn and fraught with death.

Weep for the murdered kin,
The kin who murdered him,
Dead fruits of a stubborn soul!

Weep for my son, my son
Untimely dead,
My son, whose living soul
Has stolen away in death,
My guilt, not yours.

FIRST OLD MAN

Alas, my lord, at last
You have learned where justice lies.

CREON

I have learned at last;

I hold the truth
And I am crushed by it.
On my head the gods
Have piled a steady weight
Of grief, and hurled me down
In the paths of cruelty,
Overthrowing and trampling all my joy.
Weep for all the miseries of men!

The MESSENGER *comes in from the palace.*

MESSENGER
My lord, you have this and more to bear:
Grief here in your arms, and grief besides
Inside the palace for you to see.

CREON
What greater grief could there be than this?

MESSENGER
The queen is dead, my lord, the unhappy
Mother of this corpse, dead by the sword.

CREON
O Death,
Insatiable, implacable,
The harbour of all,
What more is there to suffer?
I died with Haimon's death,
And now there is new grief,
Fresh misery to pierce the heart,
Another death to die.

(*to the* MESSENGER)

Tell me again –
The queen is dead,
Slaughter on slaughter heaped,
Another grief to bear.

MESSENGER
See for yourself. Nothing's hidden now.

The palace doors are opened, revealing EURYDICE*'s body.* CREON *gives a huge, uncontrolled cry of grief.*

CREON
A second blow!

What fate awaits me now?
See, here in my arms
The corpse that was once my son,
And there, inside,
His unhappy mother. Weep for them!

MESSENGER

Two deaths she mourned, as the sword
Drank her blood beside the altar
And night darkened her eyes in death:
Her elder son Megareus, dead in the fighting,
And Haimon his unhappy brother.
She wept for them, and with her dying breath
She cursed you, my lord, their murderer.

CREON

My heart flutters with anguish.
Will no one take a sword
And kill me too?
I am racked with pain,
Twisted and racked with grief.

MESSENGER

You stand accused of the double murder
Of your own sons. Those were her dying words.

CREON

Tell me the manner of her death again.

MESSENGER

When she heard how Haimon died, she took
A sword and drove it home, into her stricken heart.

CREON

Alas! No other man
Is guilty. I killed them,
I ended their sweet lives.
I too am dead,
And must be taken away forever.

FIRST OLD MAN

That way is best, if any way is best.
We must end things quickly now.

CREON

O Death, come down
And end my life . . .
Come now . . . no more
To bear . . . no more . . .

FIRST OLD MAN

We cannot see the future. Our care is for
The present: the future lies in other hands.

CREON

I have prayed my prayers: now and forever.

FIRST OLD MAN

There's no more need for prayer. Your fate
Is fixed; there is no escape from destiny.

CREON

Then take me away from here!
An empty husk, a father
Whose blindness killed his son,
A husband who killed his wife.
Where shall I go? Where ask
For help? For all I had
Is turned to water in my hands.
Fate crushes me. Take me away!

FIRST OLD MAN

The greatest part of happiness
Is wisdom, and reverence
For all that concerns the gods.
Ambition and mortal pride
Must always pay the price:
This is the wisdom
We learn when we are old.

Philoctetes

The legend

Philoctetes, son of of Poias king of Malis, did a favour for Heracles: he lit the funeral pyre which was to carry the hero up to Olympus to become a god. As a reward, Heracles left him his sacred bow, and a quiver of arrows that never missed.

Philoctetes joined the Greek army that went to fight in the Trojan War. On the way, he led them to the shrine of the goddess Chryse to sacrifice. But he set foot in a part of the shrine forbidden to mortals, and was bitten in the foot by its guardian, a sacred snake. The foot was poisoned, and the gods made its stench so foul, and Philoctetes' groans and cries so unbearable, that the Greek leaders sent him away from the army, and marooned him on the island of Lemnos.

The war went on for some years, and many famous heroes were killed, Achilles amongst them. But neither side won any advantage. Then a captured Trojan prophet, Helenus, revealed to the Greeks that the gods would not allow Troy to be captured, except by means of Philoctetes and his unerring bow and arrows. Odysseus went to Lemnos to fetch him, taking with him Neoptolemos, the young son of Achilles (famed as the noblest and most honest of all the Greeks). The mission succeeded; Philoctetes' wound was healed, and Troy finally fell.

The play

Out of this legend, Sophocles concentrates on a single incident: the persuading of Philoctetes to leave his island and go back to Troy. His play is partly a study of the character of Neoptolemos, a noble young man who has to choose whether or not to place loyalty to his fellow-Greeks before his own conscience.

The other main theme of the play is a favourite of Sophocles: the conflict between political morality (the way men behave to each other) and religious morality (the way men behave to the gods and to their own consciences). Sophocles is particularly interested in three ways of making other people do what you want: force, persuasion and trickery.

In the discussion of matters of political morality, the leading figure (apart from Neoptolemos) is Odysseus. For the purposes of this play he is not the noble, long-suffering hero of Homer's *Odyssey*. Instead, he is a cunning, wily trickster, a 'political' man for whom the end justifies the means, the 'lord of deceit' who later in the story of Troy devised the trick of the wooden horse.

So far as religious morality is concerned, the gods affect everyone and everything in the play. In particular, they make the stench of Philoctetes' wound, the hideous, inhuman cries he utters, so foul and unbearable that no human (hardly even Philoctetes himself) knows how to deal with them at all. Philoctetes' wound is no joke: as the scene of his collapse shows, it is a hideous, supernatural affliction, and dealing with it is like coming to terms with the gods themselves.

Philoctetes was first produced in 409 B.C. when Sophocles was over eighty years old.

Philoctetes

CHARACTERS

ODYSSEUS
NEOPTOLEMOS
PHILOCTETES
TRADER, a disguised servant of Odysseus
HERACLES

SAILORS
CHORUS OF SAILORS FROM NEOPTOLEMOS' SHIP

A deserted, barren seashore. In the background, a cliff-face. The sound of the sea can be heard. Day.
Two travellers, ODYSSEUS *and* NEOPTOLEMOS, *come in. With them, keeping a respectful distance, is a* SERVANT *of Neoptolemos.*

ODYSSEUS

This is the coast of Lemnos, a barren island
In the midst of empty sea. No one lives here.
Look, Neoptolemos, son of Achilles, son
Of the noblest of the Greeks: this is the place
I chose to maroon him, years ago –
Philoctetes of Malis, son of Poias.

I was obeying orders from our generals.
His foot was festering, oozing pus
From a foul wound. Even at festivals
We hardly dared touch the wine or meat:
He gave us no peace; day and night, he filled
The whole camp with groans and curses, cries
Of ill omen that spoiled the sacrifice.

But no more of that now. If he hears us,
If he finds out we are here, the plan
I have made to capture him will fail.
Your part is to help me. Look around
Till you find a cave with two entrances –
Two suntraps to sit in when it is cold,

And a passage between them, to sleep in
In summer, cooled by the breeze. Below it,
On the left, you should find a spring
Of fresh water, if it has not dried up.
Go quietly. Signal if he is there.
Then I'll tell you what we must do next.

NEOPTOLEMOS *explores, perhaps climbing a path up the cliff. He calls back to* ODYSSEUS.

NEOPTOLEMOS
Odysseus, sir! This *is* the right place.
I think I can see the cave you mean.

ODYSSEUS
Where is it? Above you, or further down?

NEOPTOLEMOS
Up here. Deserted, silent. No one is here.

ODYSSEUS
Look inside. He may be inside, asleep.

NEOPTOLEMOS
It's empty. There's no one about.

ODYSSEUS
Does anyone live there? Are there signs of that?

NEOPTOLEMOS
Yes: a bed of leaves, where someone sleeps.

ODYSSEUS
Is there anything else? Go further in.

NEOPTOLEMOS
A cup, roughly carved from a block of wood –
Not by a craftsman. And twigs, for a fire.

ODYSSEUS
This must be the cave. He must live here.

NEOPTOLEMOS *comes down, pointing off to one side.*

ODYSSEUS
This is the cave. He can't be far away.
A sick man, crippled by that old wound –
He couldn't get far. He's gone foraging,
For food, or some soothing herb he knows.
Leave your servant up there to stand on guard,

In case Philoctetes takes us by surprise.
He'd like to catch me, more than any Greek alive.

NEOPTOLEMOS *makes a sign to the* SERVANT, *who leaves.*

NEOPTOLEMOS
He's gone further up. He'll guard the path.
Now, lord Odysseus, what must we do next?

ODYSSEUS
Son of Achilles, I'm asking you
For courage first, and then obedience.
Whatever I tell you, however strange,
You must do it at once. That's why you came.

NEOPTOLEMOS
What must I do?

ODYSSEUS
You must cheat Philoctetes,
And tangle his soul in a net of words.
He'll ask who you are, where you are from.
Begin with the truth: you are Neoptolemos,
Son of Achilles. Then say you are sailing home,
Away from the Greeks, in a furious rage.
They begged you, persuaded you to go to Troy;
Only then, they said, could they hope to win.
But when you asked them for your father's arms –
The armour of Achilles, yours by right –
They refused, and gave it to Odysseus.

Tell him that. Call me any names you like.
Spare me no insults. He must believe you,
Or else you bring ruin on all the Greeks.
For we must have his bow;
Without it, you'll never capture Troy.

Are you surprised that he'll believe *you*,
Trust *you*, rather than me? This is the reason.
You took no part in the first expedition;
You are your own free man; you are not bound
By oaths of loyalty; you sailed with us
Of your own free will. For me, none of that
Is true. If he sees me, and has the bow,

He'll kill us both. The bow gives him power
That no one else can match. Force is useless.
That's why you must trick him, and steal the bow.

My dear boy, I know how unused you are
To this talk of stealing and trickery.
But the prize is worth it – the fall of Troy!
Take the risk. The future will prove us right.
For one little day, for one dishonest hour,
Do as I say. When it is done, your life
Can be the noblest the world has ever seen.

NEOPTOLEMOS

My lord Odysseus, even to talk of it
Is painful. How can I ever do it?
I am Achilles' son, noblest of Greeks –
How can I cheat and steal to get my way?
I'll conquer by force, not trickery.
The man is outnumbered, a poor cripple –
If he fights, he'll lose. I know
I was sent to help you, to obey you;
But with respect, my lord, I'd rather
Fight fair and lose than cheat to win.

ODYSSEUS

So like your father! When I was a young man
I was just like you: action, not argument.
But now I have learned from experience
That blows sometimes miss; words always win.

NEOPTOLEMOS

Have you more orders – or is lying enough?

ODYSSEUS

Your orders are these: play a trick, and win.

NEOPTOLEMOS

And if I persuade him without a trick?

ODYSSEUS

You won't. Persuasion, just like force, will fail.

NEOPTOLEMOS

Is he so dangerous? Has he such power?

ODYSSEUS

He has arrows of death that never miss.

NEOPTOLEMOS

To speak to him at all is dangerous.

ODYSSEUS
Not if you trick him. There is no other way.

NEOPTOLEMOS
But . . . to lie! How can you approve of that?

ODYSSEUS
If we lie, we're safe. I approve of that.

NEOPTOLEMOS
I must look him in the face, and lie to him?

ODYSSEUS
It's for your own good. Remember that.

NEOPTOLEMOS
What good will it do me, if he comes to Troy?

ODYSSEUS
With his bow, and his arrows, Troy will fall.

NEOPTOLEMOS
The oracle said that I would capture Troy.

ODYSSEUS
Using his weapons, yes. Without them, no.

NEOPTOLEMOS
We must take him, then. There is no other choice.

ODYSSEUS
Do it, and you'll win a double prize.

NEOPTOLEMOS
What prize? Knowing that, I might not still refuse.

ODYSSEUS
To be called noble and wise: that is the prize.

NEOPTOLEMOS
Very well. I refuse no longer. I agree.

ODYSSEUS
You understand clearly what you have to do?

NEOPTOLEMOS
It's clear enough. I understand.

ODYSSEUS
Stay here, then, and wait for him. I'll go:
He must not see me with you. Your servant
Up there must come back to the ship with me.
If things go slowly here, I'll send him back
Disguised as a ship's captain, to help the trick.
We'll find some clever tale for him to tell –
And whatever he says, go along with it,
Make use of it. I'll go now, back to the ship.

The rest is up to you. And may Hermes
God of trickery guide us, with Athene,
Goddess of victory, who watches over me.

ODYSSEUS *leaves. The* CHORUS *of* SAILORS *now comes in. They seem fearful and uncertain. Sometimes they speak separately, sometimes together. Parts of what they say are accompanied by music and choral movement.*

A SAILOR
Sir, we are strangers, in a strange land.
If we meet that sharp, suspicious man,
Tell us what to hide, and what to say.

ANOTHER
Princes, who rule in Zeus' name,
Are gifted more than other men:
They're subtle, they decide, they know.

ANOTHER
Sir, you are a prince, with royal power
Inherited from kings of long ago.
Tell us your orders. We will obey.

NEOPTOLEMOS
Look around now: he's not here.
This is his lair, on the island's edge.
Look your fill. But when he comes back,
The outlaw, the castaway,
Keep hidden and watch, in case
I signal suddenly for help.

FIRST SAILOR
Sir, we'll protect you, keep an eye
On you, as we have always done.
Your safety's our first concern.

SECOND SAILOR
Tell us this first: where does he live?
Where should we look? We must take care:
He may be hiding, waiting to attack.

THIRD SAILOR
Show us his haunts, his tracks,
His lair. Does he sleep rough,
Or under cover? Tell us where to look.

NEOPTOLEMOS
Look, up there: a nest in the rock,
Two entrances –
FIRST SAILOR
Poor wretch. Is he inside?
NEOPTOLEMOS
He'll be out hunting,
Shuffling in pain along these paths,
Shooting deadly arrows:
Soul-sick, they say, with pain,
With gnawing agony
No one will cure.
SAILORS
We pity him.
He is alone, and full of pain.
There is no one
To talk to him or care for him.
He is eaten with pain,
Baffled by each new day.
How can he bear it?
He is mortal: his fate
Was chosen by the gods.
Weep for the miseries of men,
Whose burden is endless pain.

Was he rich?
A nobleman's son, perhaps,
Second to none?
Now he's nothing: alone
With the beasts of woods and hills.
He is starving,
Twisted with pain.
How can he bear it?
No one hears his bitterness:
Only Echo, chuckling in the hills,
Answers his cries.
NEOPTOLEMOS
His sufferings are nothing strange.
I know they were sent by the gods.
He was marooned here alone
To soothe the savage rage

Of Chryse, and fulfil the plans
The gods made for Troy. His arrows
Are deadly: no one can escape.
When the time comes, Troy will fall
By them – and it is Heaven's will
That until then, he must stay here.

FIRST SAILOR
Listen!

NEOPTOLEMOS
What is it?

FIRST SAILOR
I heard a groan,
The groan of a man in pain.
From this side. No, this.
There it is again. A man
Dragging himself along,
Moaning with pain. A sick man,
A cripple. It's plain enough.
My lord –

NEOPTOLEMOS
What is it?

FIRST SAILOR
Think what to do:
He's nearly here. Listen:
This is no shepherd
Whistling as he goes along –
It's a man in torment,
Groaning, stumbling
His way on an empty shore.

The groans and shuffling steps come nearer, and the CHORUS *draws back.* PHILOCTETES *hobbles in, leaning on a tall, curved bow. He is ragged and sick, but still a man to be respected as much as pitied.*

PHILOCTETES
Strangers!
Who are you? Where have you come from? Why
Have you put in here, to this empty place?
There is nothing here: no shelter, no people.
What country are you from? What race of men?

From your clothes, you look like Greeks,
The most welcome sight in all the world.

If only you'd speak. Don't be afraid.
I look like a savage beast, more than a man.
Pity me. An outlaw, a castaway.
Alone, in pain. If you mean me no harm,
If you're my friends, speak to me. Answer,
Please answer. I ask for nothing else.

NEOPTOLEMOS
Of course I'll answer. And first of all,
The words you most hoped to hear: we are Greeks.

PHILOCTETES
No words are more welcome in all the world.
Greeks! After all these years . . . and you are Greeks!
My boy . . . my dear boy . . . why have you come here?
Is there something here you want? Something you need?
Or were you blown off course, in a lucky storm?
O my boy, answer me. Tell me who you are.

NEOPTOLEMOS
I come from the island of Scyros.
I am sailing home. My name is Neoptolemos,
Son of Achilles. There: you know it all.

PHILOCTETES
Achilles' son? I was his dearest friend.
I loved Scyros. I knew your guardian, too,
When your father left for Troy. But why
Have you come here? Where did your journey start?

NEOPTOLEMOS
In Troy. I am sailing home from Troy.

PHILOCTETES
How can that be? You were not with us then,
Years ago, when our army left for Troy.

NEOPTOLEMOS (*pretending surprise*)
When our army left . . . ? You mean *you* were at Troy?

PHILOCTETES
Don't you know me? Don't you recognise me?

NEOPTOLEMOS
How could I recognise a man I've never met?

PHILOCTETES
Have you never heard my name? Never heard
Of the wrongs I suffer, the pain I bear?

NEOPTOLEMOS
No. Everything you say is new to me.
PHILOCTETES
O gods! Is there more? More misery to bear?
Ten years twisted with pain – and no one knows
How I suffer, no one in the whole of Greece!
My wound feeds and grows stronger every day –
Is it still a secret, a private joke
To the criminals, cursed by the gods, who left me here?

Neoptolemos, son of Achilles:
I think you have heard of me. I am the man
Who was made master of the bow of Heracles –
Philoctetes, son of Poias. I am the man
Our generals and Odysseus of Ithaca
Banished to this empty place, the man gnawed
By a vicious sickness, marked out for death
By the murderous fangs of a deadly snake.

They left me to endure it: here, alone.
They sailed away and left me. We had come
From the island of Chryse – a hard voyage
In stormy seas. I was exhausted,
And fell asleep in a cave here on the headland.
At once, overjoyed, they seized their chance
And sailed. Oh, they left me a supply of rags,
Beggar's rags, and a little store of food.
God curse them! God send them the same one day!

Can you imagine what it was like to wake up
And find them gone? Can you imagine my tears,
My despair? The warfleet I took to Troy,
Stolen away; its captain marooned, alone,
A helpless cripple racked with pain. I looked
For a living soul to help. I searched the island.
There was no one. Nothing. All I had was pain.

So the years passed: season after season.
No one came. I am the master; I am the slave.
I just keep alive. When my belly needs food,
The bow provides it: birds, caught on the wing.
The arrows never miss, but whatever I shoot
I have to fetch myself, crawling, dragging

This foot. Sometimes in winter the pools freeze:
If I want water to drink, I must light
A fire. Then I must crawl to fetch wood,
And if the old embers are dead, grind stones
On stones to unlock the secret spark.
Shelter, and fire. I keep alive. What more
Do I need, but an end to my endless pain?

My boy, do you know what this island is like?
No sailors land here by choice. Why should they?
There are no harbours, no markets, no towns.
A sensible traveller keeps well away.

But now and then, as the years pass, men put in here
By accident. When they do, they pity me –
Or so they say. They leave me charity:
A little food, say, or some cast-off clothes.
But that other thing, when I mention it –
To be taken home – they never give me that.

A living death. I have been here ten years.
I pine, I starve, only my sickness thrives.
This is the handiwork of the sons of Atreus
And of proud Odysseus. May the gods above
Punish them one day with suffering like mine.

FIRST SAILOR

Like everyone else who comes here
I pity you, Philoctetes, I pity you.

NEOPTOLEMOS

The sons of Atreus! Proud Odysseus!
Every word you say is true. I know
Their arrogance. Their evil has touched me too.

PHILOCTETES

They are evil men, cursed by the gods.
How have they harmed you? What debt do they owe?

NEOPTOLEMOS

A debt of suffering they will pay in full.
Mycenae and Sparta will learn, one day,
That Scyros, too, breeds fighting men.

PHILOCTETES

Well said, boy! Good. But why do you hate them?
Tell me. What lodged such fury in your heart?

NEOPTOLEMOS
I'll tell you, hard though it is: how I came
To Troy, and how they mocked and insulted me.
When Fate decreed Achilles had to die –

PHILOCTETES
What? Achilles, dead? Tell me clearly:
Achilles son of Peleus, your father, is dead?

NEOPTOLEMOS
Yes, he is dead – and by no mortal hand.
They say Apollo killed him, the archer god.

PHILOCTETES
His will be done. And now, Neoptolemos
Son of Achilles, what should I do? Listen
To your story, or weep for your father's death?

NEOPTOLEMOS
Already you have cause enough to weep
For your own sake. You need not weep for him.

PHILOCTETES
What you say is true. I accept it. Tell me, then:
How did those noble lords insult you?

NEOPTOLEMOS
They came to fetch me from Scyros, in a ship
Fluttering with flags: noble Odysseus
And Phoinix, my father's old guardian.
They said – and it could have been true or false –
That with my father dead, the gods had decreed
That I, and only I, was to capture Troy.

That was their story. They soon persuaded me
To sail with them. There were two reasons. First,
My father, the father I had never seen.
His body was laid out for burial:
I wanted to touch him and weep for him.
And second, I was flattered. To think
That I, and I alone, was to capture Troy!

So we set sail. Wind and the sailors' oars
Brought us in two days to cruel Sigeum.
I went ashore. The soldiers crowded round
To welcome me. 'He's Achilles!' they said,
'He's Achilles come to life again!'

But Achilles my father was dead, laid out
For burial. I mourned him as custom demands.
Then I went to the sons of Atreus, my friends
(Or so I thought), and asked for my father's arms
And whatever else was his. For answer
They laughed at me, laughed in my face, and said,
'The arms of Achilles! Everything else
Is yours to take. But his arms have been given
To another man: to Odysseus, Laertes' son.'
Tears of fury burned my eyes. I leapt up,
Blazing, and shouted at them, 'How dare you?
How dare you give my arms to another man
Without my leave? How dare you insult me so?'
At that Odysseus said – he was standing by –
'Now now, my boy. The arms are mine by right.
I earned them when I saved your father's life.'

I was furious. I cursed him. I called down
Every insult I knew. That he should steal my arms!
He's a mild man, but at last I stung him
Into answering. 'Your place was here with us,
Fighting the Trojans – and you stayed away.
Insult me how you like, boast how you like,
You'll never sail home and take those arms.'

So, insulted and mocked, empty-handed,
I am sailing home. Odysseus took from me
What was rightly mine. The lord Odysseus!
Lord of deceit. And what of them, the generals,
The commanders, the sons of Atreus?
As a city looks to its king, so men
In battle look to their generals to lead them well.
If the man's corrupt, the master is to blame.

That's my story. Whoever hates
The sons of Atreus is my friend,
And the gods' friend, for evermore.

SAILORS

Mother Earth,
Mother of Zeus himself;
Queen of the wide river,
Pactolus of golden sands;

You ride in majesty,
Your chariot drawn
By a team of hunting lions.

Earth-mother, Queen,
I called you to witness then,
When the sons of Atreus in their pride
Over-ruled this man,
When they gave his father's arms,
A wonder of the world,
To Odysseus, Laertes' son.

PHILOCTETES

Neoptolemos, you bring a convincing tale
Of lies and insults. Everything you say
Fits what I know of them, the sons of Atreus
And Odysseus lord of deceit, who bends
His tongue to any lie, any trick
Right or wrong, that will bring him what he wants.
I know them: I'm not surprised. But where
Was Ajax? He is an honest man: he
Could have stopped them. Why didn't he speak up?

NEOPTOLEMOS

Ajax is dead. If he'd been still alive
I'd not have been robbed; I'd have the arms.

PHILOCTETES

Ajax, dead? Have the gods taken him as well?

NEOPTOLEMOS

Yes, he is dead. He lies in the underworld.

PHILOCTETES

Why should he die, and not those criminals?
Diomedes son of Tydeus, Odysseus –
Why don't they die? They should never have lived.

NEOPTOLEMOS

They live and thrive. They are princes of men,
The glory of all the fighting-men of Greece.

PHILOCTETES

And Nestor, King of Pylos – what news of him?
He was an old friend, a good, honest man.
His wise advice often stopped their wickedness.

NEOPTOLEMOS

He too has suffered. He has lost his son,
Antilochus, who sailed with him to Troy.

PHILOCTETES
Antilochus too! You have told me of the deaths
Of two good friends. What is left for us now,
What can we hope for, if Antilochus
And Ajax, who should have lived, are dead,
And Odysseus, who should be dead, still lives?

NEOPTOLEMOS
He's a skilful wrestler, who has survived
Till now. But even skilful wrestlers fall.

PHILOCTETES
In god's name, Neoptolemos! Was Patroclus
Not there to help you? Your father's dearest friend.

NEOPTOLEMOS
He is dead too. And it is always so,
Philoctetes – the wicked never die
In war, except by chance. Only good men die.

PHILOCTETES
In that case, give me news of one wicked man:
That vile creature with the clever tongue,
So expert in arguing. Is he alive?

NEOPTOLEMOS
I don't understand. Do you mean Odysseus?

PHILOCTETES
Not Odysseus, no. There was another one.
His name was Thersites. No one could stop him
Talking and arguing. Is he still alive?

NEOPTOLEMOS
I don't know him. I've not heard he is dead.

PHILOCTETES
Nothing evil has died, in this whole war.
The gods in their wisdom look after them;
It pleases them; they close the gates of Hades
To cheats and criminals, as if there was room
In the underworld only for honest men.
How can we understand? How can we praise
The gods, if we cannot praise the things they do?

NEOPTOLEMOS
Philoctetes, my part in this is done.
From now on I'll watch the Trojan War
And the sons of Atreus from far away.
Now that honest men are dead and liars thrive,

Now that heroes are beaten and cowards rule,
I'll not stay to see it: I'll go back
To stony Scyros, and live content at home.

Now I must go to the ship. Philoctetes,
I leave you with the blessing of the gods.
May they answer your prayers, and cure your sickness.
Men, we must go. When the gods send fair wind,
We must be ready to set sail at once.

PHILOCTETES

Neoptolemos! Will you go so soon?

NEOPTOLEMOS

Yes. The wind's freshening. It's time.
We must go on board, and make ready at once.

PHILOCTETES

Neoptolemos, I beg you, in the name
Of your father and mother, and all you hold dear
At home, I beg you, don't leave me here
Alone. You've seen how I suffer. You've heard
All the miseries I endure. Pity me.
Find a corner of your heart and pity me.

I know I'm not the cargo you would choose
To have on board – but bear me, put up with me!
You're a good man. Be kind, not cruel. Think
How your honour will suffer if you leave me here,
The glory and fame if you take me home.

I'll not trouble you long: less than one day.
Take me to the ship, and stow me where you like –
The stern, the hold, the prow, out of the way,
Wherever I will least offend the crew.

Say yes. I beg you in god's name, say yes.
Do as I ask. Look: I am on my knees,
A sick man, a cripple. Don't leave me here,
Marooned alone in this desert. Pity me,
Take me to Scyros, home with you, or else
To the mainland, to Euboea, from where
It is just a little step home for me
To the hills of Trachis, the plain of Spercheius.
Home! To my dear father, if he's still alive.
I have sent him so many messages
By passing travellers: prayers to come himself

Or send a ship and crew to rescue me.
But no one came. He's dead, perhaps, or else
(And I think it more likely) my messengers
Cared nothing for me, and made their own way home.

Now you have come: messenger, rescuer, all
In one. I beg you, save me, pity me.
Remember, chance governs all human life.
When it's good, when we're up, we must look out
For trouble ahead, or we may come crashing down.

SAILORS

Pity him, sir. He has told
Of unbearable suffering.
Pray god none of those we love
Ever has to suffer so.
If you hate them, sir,
The cruel sons of Atreus,
Turn the evil they have done
To this man to good.
Take him on board;
Take him swiftly home
Where he so longs to be.
Pity him, sir –
Help him, and be spared
The anger of the gods.

NEOPTOLEMOS

It's easy now to stand by and pity him.
But once he's on board, when you're sick of the stench
Of his wound, will you be so generous then?

FIRST SAILOR

Yes, sir. We understand, we accept him.
We'll not change. No one will blame us for that.

NEOPTOLEMOS

When my men are so kind, so generous,
How can I refuse? If you agree, we sail.
Philoctetes, we'll take you on board.
Go to the ship, as quickly as you can.

O gods, grant us a safe journey – safe
Passage from here, a safe voyage home.

PHILOCTETES

O blessed light of day. O dear boy . . .
Dear friends . . . how can I prove my gratitude?

Let us go, at once. Let us kiss goodbye
To this place, this dreadful place. I called it home.
Home! How did I bear it? Look for yourself –
The sight alone would frighten other men,
But I had to endure it; I had no choice;
Long suffering taught me patience in the end.

FIRST SAILOR
Look, my lords: two men, coming from the ship.
One of the crew, sir, and another man,
A stranger. What is it? We must wait, and hear.

Two men come in. One is a SAILOR. *The other is Neoptolemos' servant from the beginning of the play. He is dressed as a* TRADER.[8]

TRADER
Son of Achilles, I found this man on guard,
With two others, beside your ship. I asked him
To tell me where you were, to bring me here.
It was a lucky accident that I found you,
That I happened to anchor here in this bay.

I am the captain of a small merchant-ship.
I am sailing from Troy to Peparethos
To pick up a cargo of wine. When this man said
That he and the others were sailors of yours,
I decided to come and tell you the news –
As much as I know – news you may thank me for.

Of course, I could have sailed on without a word.
But you know nothing of what is happening,
What the Greek generals are planning to do –
No, more than planning: what they are doing now.

NEOPTOLEMOS
Thank you for your kindness, sir. I'll not
Be ungrateful. What is it? What is your news?

TRADER
They are sending warships to fetch you back.
Phoinix is in command, and Theseus' sons.

NEOPTOLEMOS
To fetch me back? By persuasion, or force?

TRADER
My lord, I cannot say. I've told you all I know.

NEOPTOLEMOS
Phoinix, and Theseus' sons. The orders came
From the generals themselves, the sons of Atreus?
TRADER
My lord, they're on their way. They'll soon be here.
NEOPTOLEMOS
Where was Odysseus? Why was he so slow
To volunteer? He can't have been afraid!
TRADER
When I left port, he had already sailed
With Diomedes, to fetch another man.
NEOPTOLEMOS
Oh yes? And who has Odysseus gone to fetch?
TRADER
His name was – no! Wait! Who is that man there?
Lower your voice; whisper. Don't let him hear.
NEOPTOLEMOS
He is the famous Philoctetes, son of Poias.
TRADER
No more, then! Ask me no more! Get clear away
From the island, clear away while you still can!
PHILOCTETES
Neoptolemos, what is it? Who is this man?
What are you bargaining behind my back?
NEOPTOLEMOS
He has more to say. And whatever it is,
He can say it openly, for us both to hear.
TRADER
Neoptolemos, no! I'm a poor man, sir;
I make my living supplying the army;
If you tell them . . . if they get to hear of it . . .
NEOPTOLEMOS
I am the sworn enemy of the sons of Atreus.
He hates them too, and therefore is my friend.
You came to do me a kindness. Do it, then:
Don't hide what you know. Tell us everything.
TRADER
Take care, my lord.
NEOPTOLEMOS
I'm not afraid of them.

TRADER
It was your own choice.
NEOPTOLEMOS
It was my own choice. Speak.
TRADER
It's this. The two men I told you of,
Lord Odysseus and Diomedes son of Tydeus –
This is the man they have sailed to fetch.
The whole Greek army heard Odysseus swear
To bring him back, by persuasion or force.
He made a solemn promise, before the gods:
He is sure of himself, more than any other man.
NEOPTOLEMOS
What made them turn their minds to him,
The generals, after all these years? How can
He help them now? They marooned him, banished him –
What do they want with him now? Have the gods
Who punish wickedness stirred them at last?
TRADER
I'll tell you, everything as it happened.
There was a noble prophet, Helenus,
Son of King Priam of Troy. One dark night
The man no good is ever spoken of,
Odysseus, went out alone and captured him
By trickery. A glittering prize! He brought
Him back, and showed him to all the Greeks.

Then Helenus began to prophesy.
Of all the things he told them, this was the first:
The city of Troy, he said, would never be theirs
Unless they could persuade this man, Philoctetes,
To leave the island and go back to them.

When he heard that, Odysseus said at once
That he was the man to do it: he would fetch
Philoctetes back, and parade him there
For everyone to see. He thought the man
Would come back by choice; but if not, he said,
He would bring him by force. And if he failed
He would forfeit his own life, his own neck.

There, Neoptolemos, you have heard it all.

I advise you to get away now, at once –
You and anyone else you care about.

PHILOCTETES

So he's sworn to persuade me back? To parade me
In front of them? Odysseus, the plague of Greece!
If I was dead, a corpse in the underworld,
He'd not persuade me back. He will not now.

TRADER

Well, that's as may be. I must go back, now,
To my ship. May the gods send you all you need.

He goes.

PHILOCTETES

Does he really think he can persuade me back?
Does he think he can gentle me with words
Into that ship, back to those Greeks? No!
Sooner than him, I'd listen to the snake
That destroyed me, that poisoned away my foot.
But he'll say anything, dare anything.
Neoptolemos, hurry. He'll soon be here.
A whole ocean must separate our ships.
Let us go, now: haste when the time is right
Eases the journey, brings peace and rest at last.

NEOPTOLEMOS

No, we must wait for the wind. When it changes
We can sail. It's blowing against us now.

PHILOCTETES

When you're running from danger, all winds help.

NEOPTOLEMOS

No. It's against us. And against them too.

PHILOCTETES

Against them? What wind has ever stopped
Pirates, criminals, from hunting their prey?

NEOPTOLEMOS

If that's what you want, we'll sail at once.
Is there anything you need, inside the cave?

PHILOCTETES

There isn't much – a few necessities.

NEOPTOLEMOS

Necessities? The ship is well supplied.

PHILOCTETES
One thing above all: a herb I have found
To poultice the wound and soften the pain.

NEOPTOLEMOS
Go and fetch it, then. Is there anything else?

PHILOCTETES
The arrows. I must count them, and check that none
Have been left for anyone else to find.

NEOPTOLEMOS
Is that the famous bow, there in your hand?

PHILOCTETES
There are no others. Yes, this is the bow.

NEOPTOLEMOS
May I look at it closer? The bow of the gods!
May I handle it, and pay it my respects?

PHILOCTETES
My dear boy, you know that it, and all I have,
Are at your service. You have only to ask.

NEOPTOLEMOS
Only to ask . . . If what I want is right
In the eyes of the gods, I'll ask for it.
But if it's wrong – well then, let it go.

PHILOCTETES
You're right to respect the gods. What you ask
Is allowed. You have given me back my life;
You are taking me home to my native land,
To my dear father and the friends I love;
My enemies trampled me – you have raised me up.

Take the bow. Touch it, handle it. Now
Give it back. There. Now you can boast
That you and I are the only living men
To touch it. It is a reward for kindness:
My kindness to another, and now yours to me.

NEOPTOLEMOS
My dear friend, thank you. A man who understands
How to reward kindness with kindness – that man
Is a friend beyond price. Now, go inside.

PHILOCTETES
Come with me. Help me. Let me lean on your arm.

He stumbles out, leaning on NEOPTOLEMOS' *arm.*

Music. The SAILORS *move and speak (sometimes separately, sometimes together).*

SAILORS

One other, one other only,
Has suffered so:
Ixion, bound to a wheel of fire.
He slept with Hera, Zeus' queen,
And he was punished.
But this man is innocent:
All his life he has lived
With justice among the just.
Why has he deserved such pain?

How has he endured such pain,
A life of tears, alone
By the breakers on the shore?
There was no one else: no one
To hear the cripple's groans
As the sickness gnawed him;
No one to gather soothing herbs
When scalding pus oozed
From his ulcers, his gangrened foot.
He crept, he crawled
Like a helpless child
Torn from its nurse's arms.

When the jaws of his pain
Parted a little, and set him free,
He crept out to look for food.

No seeds were his, no fruits
Of the bountiful earth,
Such as industrious men
Gather and store.
His was the meagre prey
His bow brought down
To feed his belly then.

First hunger, then thirst:
For ten long years
No taste of the wine
That brings men joy.

Instead, when he spied
A stagnant pool,
He stooped and drank.

Now he has met, at last,
A man of honour
Who will lift him up
To his old, high place.
In a fast ship
Butting the waves
He will take him home.

Home! Where nymphs play
By the river banks
Of Spercheius, and above
On the high hills
Heracles rules,
A man made god
In holy fire.

As they finish, NEOPTOLEMOS *comes in again.* PHILOCTETES *follows more slowly, hobbling in pain.*

NEOPTOLEMOS
Come on. Hurry. Why are you standing there dumb?
You're like a man thunderstruck. What's happened?

PHILOCTETES (*groaning*)
Oh! Oh!

NEOPTOLEMOS
What is it?

PHILOCTETES
It's all right. Go ahead, child.

NEOPTOLEMOS
Is it the old agony, the old wound?

PHILOCTETES
No, no. It's all right. It's better now.
O gods!

NEOPTOLEMOS
Why are you groaning, and calling on the gods?

PHILOCTETES
O gods, help me. Help me, heal me now.
Ah! Ah!

NEOPTOLEMOS
What's the matter? Tell me. If you're in such pain
Tell me. What reason is there for hiding it?

PHILOCTETES
You're right. There's no use hiding it.
I'm on the rack, Neoptolemos. The pain
Twists . . . gouges . . . tears me alive. O my child . . .

Suddenly, without warning, he gives a huge, uncontrolled scream of agony and grief. He beckons desperately to NEOPTOLEMOS, *who is both astonished and revolted by the unhuman sound.*

Neoptolemos, I beg you, in the name of god,
Draw your sword, if you have it. Cut, here . . .
Cut off this foot . . . even if I die of it . . .
Neoptolemos, please . . .

NEOPTOLEMOS
This agony, so suddenly – these groans and cries –
Is it some new attack? What has brought it on?

PHILOCTETES
O my boy . . .

NEOPTOLEMOS
Yes?

PHILOCTETES
My boy, my child . . .

NEOPTOLEMOS
What is it?

PHILOCTETES
Can't you see? Can't you understand?

NEOPTOLEMOS
I see how it tortures you.

PHILOCTETES
Tortures me . . . destroys me. Help me . . . Oh help me.

NEOPTOLEMOS
How?

PHILOCTETES
Don't leave me. Don't leave me. Don't be afraid.
The pain . . . this attack . . . the Fury settles here
From time to time . . . on me . . . then someone else . . .

NEOPTOLEMOS
Philoctetes, I pity you.

I see your suffering, and pity you.
How shall I help? Shall I lift you up?

PHILOCTETES

No. What you asked for before. Take my bow.
Take it. While the pain lasts. Keep it safe for me.
When the attack passes, I fall asleep.
The first sign that it's over. Leave me to sleep,
Don't wake me. If . . . those other men come . . .
Neoptolemos, I order you in the name of the gods,
Don't give them the bow, don't let them take it.
If you do, we both die. You murder us both,
Yourself and the man you have sworn to help.

NEOPTOLEMOS

It's all right. I'll see to it. No one but you
Or I will touch it. Give it me. Pray for good luck.

PHILOCTETES

There it is, child. Pray to the jealous gods
That they spare you pain such as they have given me,
Suffering like Heracles', who gave me the bow.

NEOPTOLEMOS

God grant these prayers. And grant us, O god,
An easy voyage with a following wind,
Safe journey, wherever our fate is leading us.

PHILOCTETES (*screaming*)

No, child, no. Look! Prayers are useless . . .
Wasted . . . Look! There, inside . . . fresh blood, fresh pus
Oozing . . . Oh, it's here again . . . Oh! Oh!
My foot . . . my jailer, my executioner . . .
It's here, it's here . . .
Oh! Oh!

Don't leave me . . .

If this were you,
Odysseus . . . if it were only you
Transfixed by this agony . . . Oh! Oh!
If only the generals . . . Agamemnon, Menelaus . . .
The sons of Atreus . . . this should be their pain . . .
Now, forever. Oh! Oh!

O death, I have called you so often –
Come down for me now. Why will you not come?

O my child, O Neoptolemos . . . my boy . . .
The fire, look! Be kind . . . pick me up, and burn me
To ashes . . . a funeral pyre. Then they will call me
The Lemnian. Please, Neoptolemos! Once I, too,
Did that kindness for Heracles, son of Zeus . . .
A kindness, a favour . . . he gave me the bow . . .
He gave me the bow for it . . . it's in your hands . . .
O Neoptolemos, answer . . .
Neoptolemos . . . Neoptolemos . . . what is it?

NEOPTOLEMOS *has turned away his head.*

NEOPTOLEMOS
I suffer for your suffering, in pain for your pain.

PHILOCTETES
Be comforted. The Fury settles a little
And then flies on. It's not long. Don't leave me . . .

NEOPTOLEMOS
It's all right. I'll stay. There's no doubt of that.

PHILOCTETES
In god's name, swear! No: I mustn't ask that.

NEOPTOLEMOS
They won't let me go without you.

PHILOCTETES
My son . . . your hand . . .

NEOPTOLEMOS
There. I will stay.

PHILOCTETES
Lift me up . . .

NEOPTOLEMOS
Where?

PHILOCTETES
Up there.

NEOPTOLEMOS
It's empty sky. What are you looking at?

PHILOCTETES
Let me go! Let me go!

NEOPTOLEMOS
What is it?

PHILOCTETES
Don't touch me! I'm dying. Don't touch me!

NEOPTOLEMOS
Calm . . . calm . . . There.

PHILOCTETES (*on the ground*)
O earth, mother earth, receive me. I'm dying.
I'll never stand up again. Twisted . . . a cripple . . . sick . . .

NEOPTOLEMOS
His head is drooping. Soon, he will sleep.
He's covered in sweat; a dark trickle
Of clean blood is running from his foot.
Leave him now. Leave him to sleep in peace.

SAILORS (*as* PHILOCTETES *sleeps*)
Sleep that knows no pain,
No suffering, answer our prayers.
Breathe over us, blessed lord.
His eyes are closed:
Breathe over him rest and peace.
Come, sleep, and heal his pain.

FIRST SAILOR
Now, sir, see where you stand.
What's to be done? What plan
Is best? The man's asleep:
What are we waiting for?
We know what to do –
We must do it, now.

NEOPTOLEMOS
He can't hear us. The bow is a glittering prize –
But without him, if we sail without him, it's nothing.
His is the crown; the gods say he must be fetched;
How can we leave it half-done – and that half by lies?

FIRST SAILOR
Sir, you must leave that to the gods.
And, sir, you must speak softly,
You must whisper what you say.
For a sick man's sleep
Is restless, easily disturbed –
Quick to hear, and start awake.

SECOND SAILOR
Now, sir, now it's time.
You must do what must be done.
Finish it! Win the game!
Think, sir, and you'll see

That the plan in your mind,
The other plan, will fail.

THIRD SAILOR

The wind's behind us, sir.
He can see nothing, do nothing –
Stretched out, asleep in the sun.
He doesn't move: hands, feet still.
You might think he was dead.
Sir, now it's time.
No risk, no fear –
Surely it's time.

NEOPTOLEMOS

Be quiet! Fool! Look: he's stirring.
He's opening his eyes. He's awake.

PHILOCTETES *wakes up, still dazed.*

PHILOCTETES

Bright sunlight . . . I have been asleep. And you . . .
My friends . . . you waited, against all hope.
My son . . . my dear boy . . . I'd never have dared hope
That you'd feel such pity, such friendly care . . .
That you'd wait, and help. The noble generals,
The sons of Atreus, were not so long-suffering.

You're a fine boy, the son of a noble father,
And so you put up with it: the groaning,
The sick smell, everything. You put up with it.

And now the attack is over. The pain has gone,
And the gods have given me a little rest.
Lift me up, Neoptolemos, lift me up.
When the dizziness clears and I can walk,
We'll go to the ship, and set sail at once.

NEOPTOLEMOS

So ill, and so soon recovered! My dear friend,
I'm glad. You were so tortured, at the height
Of the attack, I thought you were sure to die.
Let me help you up. Or else, if you prefer,
My men will carry you: they'll do as we say.

PHILOCTETES

Neoptolemos, thank you. Help me up:

I'll walk. I'll not trouble them yet. The smell
Of my wound will be hard enough to bear on board.

NEOPTOLEMOS
Just as you say. Stand up . . . take hold of my arm.

PHILOCTETES (*as he struggles to his feet*)
I think I'll be able to stand again . . . There.

NEOPTOLEMOS
O Zeus! How can I bear it? What shall I do?

PHILOCTETES
Neoptolemos, what is it? What do you mean?

NEOPTOLEMOS
How can I tell you? How can I explain?

PHILOCTETES
Tell me what? Explain what? I don't understand.

NEOPTOLEMOS
It's time. There's no more choice. You must be told.

PHILOCTETES
Must be told what? Is my sickness so foul,
So corrupt, that you're leaving me behind?

NEOPTOLEMOS
The corruptness, the foulness, are here in me.
I chose to do wrong. I betrayed myself.

PHILOCTETES
You helped a man who needed help. Just like
Your father! How have you betrayed yourself?

NEOPTOLEMOS
I chose to do wrong. Soon you'll understand.

PHILOCTETES
All you've done is good. Your words make me afraid.

NEOPTOLEMOS
Zeus, what can I do? To be a traitor, twice!
Shall I say nothing and hide it – or tell more lies?

PHILOCTETES
Neoptolemos, no! Surely you don't intend
To leave me here, to leave me and sail away?

NEOPTOLEMOS
If only I could! You have to come with me.
That's the truth, that's the torment I have to bear.

PHILOCTETES
What do you mean, child? I still don't understand.

NEOPTOLEMOS
Listen, then. It's this. You must sail back to Troy,
To the Greeks, to the army of the sons of Atreus . . .

PHILOCTETES
It's not true! You're lying! It must be a lie!

NEOPTOLEMOS
It's true. But listen to me . . . let me explain . . .

PHILOCTETES
Explain what? What else have you planned for me?

NEOPTOLEMOS
My orders are these: to rescue you from here
And take you back to sack the land of Troy.

PHILOCTETES
And that's why you came here? That's your plan?

NEOPTOLEMOS
Philoctetes, forgive me. I had no choice.

PHILOCTETES
No choice? Murderer! Stranger! Give me the bow!

NEOPTOLEMOS
I can't. I have my orders. I must obey.

PHILOCTETES
No fire, no monster of hell, no foul scheme
Festering in the mind of man, is worse than you.
You tricked me, you cheated me. The man you helped,
The man who trusted you. Trusted you – for this!

You have stolen my bow, my life. I beg you,
On my knees I beg you, give it back.
By the gods you hold dear, give me back my life.

No. He'll not answer. He turns away.
He'll not give it back.

O rocks, hills, lairs of the mountain beasts,
Harbours and headlands, I cry aloud to you.
There's no one else. Hear me! Hear me!
Hear what Achilles' son has done to me.

He swore he'd take me home – he's taking me
To Troy. He held out his hand – and took my bow,
My sacred bow, the gift of Heracles son of Zeus.
He wants to brandish it in front of all

The Greeks, and boast how he won it, how he captured me
In all my strength. He has overpowered a ghost,
A shadow, an empty husk. And even so
He could only win by trickery. If I'd had
My former strength, he'd never have taken me.

You tricked me, destroyed me. What shall I do?
Give it back. I beg you, give it back . . .
Be your own true self again. My boy, my child . . .

Still he won't answer. Still he looks away.
Now I have nothing. O my cave, my double cave,
Your dear master is here, unarmed, alone.
I'll come inside; I'll wither and die.
No birds on the wing, no mountain beasts, will fall
To these arrows now. I'll die, alone,
A feast of flesh for the ones I feasted on,
The prey of my prey, my blood for their blood.

He seemed so honest, so innocent of guilt.
I trusted him, and he took my life away.

Will you change your mind? Will you pity me?
Then die in misery! Die a traitor's death!

FIRST SAILOR
Sir, what shall we do? You must decide.
Shall we do as he begs us, or sail for Troy?

NEOPTOLEMOS
I am filled with a strange kind of pity.
Ever since I met him, I have pitied him.

PHILOCTETES
Have mercy, my child. In god's name, pity me.
Who'll honour you for trickery and lies?

NEOPTOLEMOS
What shall I do? What choice is left for me?
Why did I leave Scyros, and sail for Troy?

PHILOCTETES
You're not wicked: you were trained in wickedness
By those others, those criminals. Leave it to them!
Give me my bow, and sail away from here.

NEOPTOLEMOS (*to the* FIRST SAILOR)
What do you think, friend? What's your advice?

Before he can be answered, ODYSSEUS *comes in angrily.*

ODYSSEUS
Traitor! Coward! Give me the bow!

PHILOCTETES
Odysseus! Is it Odysseus?

ODYSSEUS
Odysseus, yes.

PHILOCTETES
Then I'm betrayed, I'm dead. You plotted this:
This trickery was yours, to steal the bow.

ODYSSEUS
Of course. The whole plan, every detail, was mine.

PHILOCTETES
Boy! Quickly! The bow! Give me the bow!

ODYSSEUS
He can't, whether he wants to or not. And where
The bow goes, you go. My men will see to that.

PHILOCTETES
Your men? Your men! Have you sunk so low?
Have you brought soldiers here, to lay hands on *me*?

ODYSSEUS
They're waiting. Will you come willingly, or not?

PHILOCTETES
In the name of Lemnos, forged by the hand of god!
Am I a prisoner, to be dragged away by force?

ODYSSEUS
Zeus is in command here, Zeus king of the gods.
I am only his servant. This is his will.

PHILOCTETES
Will you try to make Zeus your accomplice now?
Must he protect you? Must he lie for you?

ODYSSEUS
Zeus does not lie. He commands. We must obey.

PHILOCTETES
I will not go.

ODYSSEUS
You must. There is no other choice.

PHILOCTETES
O Zeus, was it for this that I was born?
Philoctetes son of Poias – to be a slave?

ODYSSEUS
Not so. You're not a slave. You're brave, among
The brave: Philoctetes, Sacker of Troy.

PHILOCTETES
No! I refuse! Do what you like to me.
The cliff . . . the headland, the precipice . . . let me go!

ODYSSEUS
Go? Why?

PHILOCTETES
Sooner than give way, I'll throw myself down,
And smash myself to pieces on the rocks.

ODYSSEUS
No! Hold him, both of you. Don't let him escape.

PHILOCTETES (*held imprisoned by two* SAILORS)
Hunted, netted, trapped like an animal
For want of my dear bow . . . and by Odysseus!
You can think no decent or honest thought;
You stole up on me, like a thief in the night;
You set a trap, and used this boy as bait.

What made you choose him? I didn't know him,
He was a stranger. He is like me, not you –
He believes in justice and honesty. All he did
Was obey orders, and now he is suffering:
He betrayed me, and betrayed himself as well.
He was an innocent child: your serpent's tongue,
Sharp in the shadows, taught him his trade of lies.

And now you want *me*! You marooned me here
Alone; you deserted me; you left me to die –
And now you come back, to drag me away in chains.

Die! Die by the gods!
I have prayed that prayer so often. But the gods
Are deaf. You live and laugh. And I am in pain,
A tortured wretch, lost in a sea of pain –
While you laugh, you and the sons of Atreus,
Your masters, the generals of all the Greeks.

You had to be tricked, *you* had to be forced
To accept the yoke, to sail with them to Troy.
I came willingly, *I* sailed with seven ships –
For this! To be robbed, to be thrown aside!
Was it your work or theirs? Each blames the other.

And now what will you do? Where will you take me? Why?
I am nothing. To you, I have long been dead.
Have you forgotten my foot? The stench of it?
If I come with you to Troy, how will you pray,
How will you sacrifice? Have you forgotten?
That was your excuse for leaving me here before.

Die! Die in agony!
If the gods are just, die for your crimes to me!
Are they not just? Did they not spur you on
To launch your ship, and sail to fetch me home?

O gods of my native land,
Punish them! Punish them! If you pity me,
If the time is right, rise up and punish them.
My life is torture – but if I see them dead,
If you punish them, I'll think my pain is cured.

FIRST SAILOR

Stubborn words, Odysseus – stubborn words
From a stubborn man. He'll not give way.

ODYSSEUS

I could answer him. There are many arguments.
But now is not the time. I'll say just this:
I make myself the man each occasion demands.
When honesty and justice are required,
I am the justest, most honest man alive.
But in everything I do, I fight to win.
Except this once. This once, I give way to you.

Let him go. He's free.
He can stay on the island. We have the bow –
We don't need you. Prince Teucer is with us still,
A skilled bowman – and I am there myself,
As clever as you, I think, at archery.
We don't need you. Stay here! Enjoy your island!

It's time to go. Perhaps this bow, this prize
Of his, will bring me the honour reserved for him.

PHILOCTETES

You'll take my bow? You'll take it, and flaunt
Yourself with it, in front of all the Greeks?

ODYSSEUS

There's nothing more to say. It's time to go.

PHILOCTETES
Son of Achilles, will you not answer me?
Will you sail away, and leave me without a word?

ODYSSEUS
On, Neoptolemos! So decent, so honest –
If you once look at him, we lose the game!

PHILOCTETES (*to the* CHORUS)
My friends, pity me. Don't leave me here alone.

FIRST SAILOR (*with a glance at* NEOPTOLEMOS)
We obey his orders. It's for him to say.

NEOPTOLEMOS
I know I'll be called soft-hearted, easy.
But you can do as he asks. You can stay here
While the ship's prepared, and sacrifice
Is made for a fair wind. Perhaps he'll change
His mind; perhaps he'll understand at last.

Lord Odysseus and I will go on ahead.
We'll signal when it's time. Come then, at once.

ODYSSEUS, NEOPTOLEMOS *and their sailors go.*
PHILOCTETES *and the* SAILORS *remain. Music.*

PHILOCTETES
Rock-tomb, rock-womb,
Sun-warm, ice-cold,
Home of my misery
Forever, home
Till the day I die.
Weep for me, echo my grief.
How must I live?
Where must I turn
For food, for hope
To nourish me?
To the birds above?
They fly free
On the wind's wings:
All my strength is gone.

FIRST SAILOR
You chose this fate;
You burdened yourself.
It was not imposed

By a greater power.
You had a choice,
And you chose this fate.

PHILOCTETES

Distracted with grief
And torn with pain;
A hermit, stripped
Of all living men
Till the day I die.
Stripped of my strength,
The swift arrows
That brought me food.
Dark, twisted words
Choked my mind.
If only that man,
That cunning man,
Shared all my pain,
My endless pain.

FIRST SAILOR

This is no trick,
Sir: this is fate.
We are not to blame.
Turn your curses away,
Curse someone else.
We are your friends.

PHILOCTETES

On the shore, by the grey sea,
He sits and laughs at me.
In his hands he waves my bow,
The bow of my life, the bow
That nourished me, the bow
No other man has held but me.

O my dear bow, stolen away
From the loving hands that held you,
If you could see, if you could feel,
How you would pity me:
Heracles' friend, your old master,
Your master no more.

You have a new master now,
New hands to string, to bend, to fire.

Look at his face, and see deceit,
Injustice, treachery – my enemy,
And all the teeming agony
His cunning has made for me.

FIRST SAILOR

A man should speak only the truth:
No slander, no venom of the tongue.
Odysseus was sent here, one man
By many. He was obeying orders;
What he did was a service,
A service to help his friends.

PHILOCTETES

Birds of the air; wild beasts,
Eyes gleaming in the hills
Where I hunted you, now you are safe!
Start up from your lairs and flee
No more. My hands are empty,
My weapons, my arrows, gone.

There is no more terror now,
No more danger. The island
Is yours: walk freely
Where you will. Soon
It will be time to feast,
To glut yourselves on my rotting flesh,
My blood for yours.

My life will be over soon.
Soon I will die. For where,
And how, will I find my food?
Can a man eat empty air?
Mother earth, who feeds all men,
Gives me no nourishment.

FIRST SAILOR

Come nearer: we are your friends.
What we say is good advice.
Remember: it is in your own power
To change your fate, to rid yourself
Of this burden of plague,
This suffering that eats your life.

PHILOCTETES

Must you torture me still?

Kindest of friends,
Must you open the wound
And torment me still?

FIRST SAILOR

What have we done?

PHILOCTETES

Why, why did you come?
Why did you ever hope
To take me back
To that detested Troy?

FIRST SAILOR

We think it is best.

PHILOCTETES

Leave me! Leave me now!

FIRST SAILOR

Very well. Your words
Are welcome. Let's go, men:
The ship is waiting.

PHILOCTETES

Don't go! In the name
Of the anger of Zeus, don't go!

FIRST SAILOR

Be calm.

PHILOCTETES

In god's name, wait.

FIRST SAILOR

For what?

PHILOCTETES

Pain . . . pain . . .
Demon pain . . .
Twisting, torturing . . .
My foot . . .
How can I bear it?
Why can't I die?
O my friends, come back.

FIRST SAILOR

Have you changed your mind?
What must we do?

PHILOCTETES

Don't be angry.
I was delirious.

The jagged pain . . .
I said . . . I didn't mean . . .

FIRST SAILOR

Come with us. Do as we ask.

PHILOCTETES

No! Not if Zeus himself
In a flash of white fire
Scorches me, sears me to the bone.
Topple, Troy, and crush them,
My enemies who took me,
A cripple, and left me here.
O my friends, my dear friends, if only . . .

FIRST SAILOR

What do you ask?

PHILOCTETES

Give me an axe, a sword, a spear . . .

FIRST SAILOR

What new madness . . . ?

PHILOCTETES

Head . . . arms . . . hack them,
Butcher them . . .
I must die now.

FIRST SAILOR

Why?

PHILOCTETES

I must find him . . . my father . . .

FIRST SAILOR

Where?

PHILOCTETES

In Hades . . . in the underworld,
Far from this light.
O my native land,
If only I could come home . . .
Cursed, since the day
I left the holy river, and came
To the Greeks, my enemies,
To help them. No more . . . no more . . .

He stumbles out.

FIRST SAILOR

We should have gone to the ship long ago.
But here comes Neoptolemos – and Odysseus with him.

NEOPTOLEMOS comes in. He is carrying the bow. ODYSSEUS hurries after him.

ODYSSEUS
Where are you going? Why are you hurrying back?

NEOPTOLEMOS
I did wrong before. Now I must set things right.

ODYSSEUS
You're talking nonsense. What wrong did you do?

NEOPTOLEMOS
I took orders from you and the other Greeks –

ODYSSEUS
And you call that wrong? What was wrong in that?

NEOPTOLEMOS
I used trickery and lies to cheat a man.

ODYSSEUS
What do you mean now? What madness is this?

NEOPTOLEMOS
No madness. A debt. A debt I mean to pay.

ODYSSEUS
What are you saying? You intend to give – ?

NEOPTOLEMOS
I intend to give back the bow I stole.

ODYSSEUS
You can't mean it! To give back the bow – !

NEOPTOLEMOS
I stole it, and now I intend to give it back.

ODYSSEUS
Is this a joke? In god's name, is this a joke?

NEOPTOLEMOS
It's no joke. I mean it. It's the truth.

ODYSSEUS
You're crazy! You mean it? You'll really do it?

NEOPTOLEMOS
Don't you understand? Are three times not enough?

ODYSSEUS
Yes, three times are enough. Once was enough.

NEOPTOLEMOS
Then you do understand. There's no more to say.

ODYSSEUS
You won't do it. You'll be stopped.

NEOPTOLEMOS
Stopped? Who by?

ODYSSEUS
The soldiers of Greece, and among them me.
NEOPTOLEMOS
The wise Odysseus! You talk like a fool.
ODYSSEUS
You are the fool, in all you do or say.
NEOPTOLEMOS
Fool or not, what I intend to do is just.
ODYSSEUS
Just? To give him back this prize – the prize
I helped you win?
NEOPTOLEMOS
The prize you helped me steal.
I cheated; I lied. I must set things right.
ODYSSEUS
Aren't you afraid? The army of the Greeks –
NEOPTOLEMOS
My army is justice. *You* should be afraid.
ODYSSEUS
And if I use force?
NEOPTOLEMOS
My mind is made up.
ODYSSEUS
If I forget the Trojans, and fight with *you* . . . ?
NEOPTOLEMOS
The choice is made.
ODYSSEUS
Here is my sword.
NEOPTOLEMOS
And mine. I'm ready. Will you stand, and fight?
ODYSSEUS
No, I'll not kill you. I'll go back to them,
And give them my report. They'll deal with you.
NEOPTOLEMOS
Wise Odysseus! Common sense at last!
Remember this, and keep clear of trouble.

ODYSSEUS *goes.* NEOPTOLEMOS *looks towards the cave, calling softly.*

NEOPTOLEMOS
Philoctetes. Philoctetes, son of Poias.

PHILOCTETES
Who's there? Who's calling, outside the cave?

He comes in.

Neoptolemos! What evil brings you again?
Have you brought new pain to top the old?

NEOPTOLEMOS
Don't be afraid. Listen. Hear what I say.

PHILOCTETES
I listened before. Honeyed words! I listened,
I trusted you – and you brought me to this!

NEOPTOLEMOS
And if I say I've had a change of heart?

PHILOCTETES
A change of heart? You were like this before –
Until you stole my bow. You smiled – and you lied.

NEOPTOLEMOS
I'm not lying now. I want to ask you this:
Will you stay here, endure it to the end,
Or will you sail with us?

PHILOCTETES
Enough! You waste words.
I'll not listen. I'll hear no more arguments.

NEOPTOLEMOS
Your mind is fixed?

PHILOCTETES
More firmly than you know.

NEOPTOLEMOS
If I could have persuaded you, I would.
But if all my words are wasted –

PHILOCTETES
Every one!
You can say nothing that pleases me, nothing
I want to hear. You stole my life, my bow –
And now you bring me arguments instead!
That Prince Achilles should father such a son!
Die, all of you! The sons of Atreus first,
Odysseus next, and last Neoptolemos!

NEOPTOLEMOS
You can save your curses. Here is your bow.

PHILOCTETES
What did you say? Is this another lie?
NEOPTOLEMOS
No lie. I swear by the honour of Zeus himself.
PHILOCTETES
Words of happiness . . . if only they're true . . .
NEOPTOLEMOS
They're true. This is the proof. Take your bow.

He is about to hand over the bow, when ODYSSEUS' *voice is heard from just offstage.*

ODYSSEUS
No! I forbid it, in the name of god!
For the sake of the army, for the sake
Of the sons of Atreus, give me the bow!
PHILOCTETES
Odysseus! That was Odysseus' voice.
ODYSSEUS (*off*)
Odysseus, yes. And I am here: I have come
To take you by force to the plain of Troy,
Whether Achilles' son agrees, or not.
PHILOCTETES
One arrow will stop these boasts.

He sets an arrow to the bow.

NEOPTOLEMOS
Philoctetes, no!
PHILOCTETES
Let me go, boy. In god's name, let me go.

They struggle.

NEOPTOLEMOS
I can't.
PHILOCTETES
Why did you stop me from killing him –
My enemy, the man I most hate in Greece?
NEOPTOLEMOS
Enemy or friend, he's not for us to kill.
PHILOCTETES
I tell you this: those leaders of the Greeks,

Those glib spokesmen, are brave enough with words,
But when it comes to fighting they cower, they cringe.

NEOPTOLEMOS

He's gone. You have your bow. There's no more cause
For anger. I helped you: I'm no more to blame.

PHILOCTETES

Neoptolemos, son of Achilles, you have shown
The true spirit of your father, the finest of all
The heroes of Greece, alive or among the dead.

NEOPTOLEMOS

Philoctetes, thank you. You give high praise
To my father and myself. Give one thing more:
A fair hearing for what I have to ask.
All men must bear whatever fate the gods
Allot them, good or bad – but when a man
Brings suffering on himself, and clings to it
As you do, no one forgives or pities him.

You're like a savage; you take no advice;
When someone offers you a friendly word
You spit with hate, as if he meant you harm.
Even so, I will speak. In your name, lord Zeus!
Hear what I say: imprint it on your mind.

The sickness you are suffering came from a god.
You strayed inside the sacred shrine of Chryse,
And disturbed the hidden snake, its guardian.
And now you are poisoned, you will find no cure
While the sun sets and rises, rises and sets,
Until you come to Troy of your own free will.
We have doctors there, sons of Asclepius,
And they will cure your wound. Then, with this bow,
And my help, you will topple the towers of Troy.

I'll tell you how I know that this is true.
There is a prisoner in camp, a man of Troy,
The prophet Helenus. He has prophesied
Plainly that all this will happen – and more,
That Troy will fall before this summer ends.
He'll give his life as forfeit if he lies.

You've heard it all. Give way. Do as I ask.

There are rich rewards: to be called a prince
Of princes, to find healing for your wound,
And this above all, to capture tearful Troy.

PHILOCTETES

Detested life, why do you keep me here
In the world above, and not send me down to Hades?
What can I do? Must I reject his words,
The advice of a true friend – or give way to him?
A sick man, a cripple – if I go back,
How can I face them? What can I say to them?

It's not resentment for the past that stings,
But fear of the future. I understand these men.
Once the first wickedness is hatched, their minds
Breed nothing but wickedness, nothing but crime.

And you, Neoptolemos: I don't understand.
You have every reason to stay away from Troy,
Not to persuade me back. They wronged you, too:
They plundered your father's arms – Achilles' arms! –
And gave them to Odysseus. Must you go back
And fight their battles? Must I fight too?

No, Neoptolemos! Take me home instead;
Go back to Scyros; leave those evil men
To die an evil death. If you help me now
You will earn a double blessing, a double thanks –
Mine and your father's. But if he sees you
Helping those hated men, he'll hate you too.

NEOPTOLEMOS

I hear what you say. Even so, I beg you:
Trust me, trust the gods. Sail back with me.

PHILOCTETES

To Troy, to the accursed sons of Atreus?
A helpless cripple – and King Agamemnon?

NEOPTOLEMOS

To skilful doctors who will heal your foot,
Dry up the ulcers and end your agony.

PHILOCTETES

Cunning words! You're so full of good advice!

NEOPTOLEMOS

What I advise is best – for both of us.

PHILOCTETES
The gods are listening! Are you not ashamed?
NEOPTOLEMOS
Why should I be ashamed? The advice is good.
PHILOCTETES
Good for the sons of Atreus, not for me.
NEOPTOLEMOS
Yes, for you. I am your friend. I'm helping you.
PHILOCTETES
You're betraying me, helping my enemies.
NEOPTOLEMOS
My poor friend, so stubborn, so determined to suffer.
PHILOCTETES
I hear my death in every word you say.
NEOPTOLEMOS
You refuse to listen, refuse to understand.
PHILOCTETES
This much I understand: they marooned me here.
NEOPTOLEMOS
They marooned you, and now they'll rescue you.
PHILOCTETES
I'll never agree to go back to Troy.
NEOPTOLEMOS
What can I do? You have rejected all
My arguments. Perhaps I should leave you here,
Without more words, to live the life you live
Here on the island, with no one to rescue you.
PHILOCTETES
If it has to be endured, I'll endure it.
But remember your promise, Neoptolemos:
Your promise to take me home. Oh, do it now!
Forget Troy. We've had pain and tears enough.
NEOPTOLEMOS
I agree. Let's go.
PHILOCTETES
Neoptolemos . . . you agree?
NEOPTOLEMOS
Walk with firm steps.
PHILOCTETES
As firmly as I can.

NEOPTOLEMOS
The Greeks will punish me.
PHILOCTETES
Pay them no heed.
NEOPTOLEMOS
If they attack my country . . . ?
PHILOCTETES
I will be there.
NEOPTOLEMOS
How will you help?
PHILOCTETES
With the arrows of Heracles.
NEOPTOLEMOS
You mean . . . ?
PHILOCTETES
I will drive them away.
NEOPTOLEMOS
My true friend! My ally!
Kiss Lemnos farewell; come to the ship.

They are about to leave, when the god HERACLES *appears on high. They cower back, and worship him.*

HERACLES
Stop! Philoctetes, son of Poias,
Listen to my words.
You hear, you see,
Heracles son of Zeus.
From the high place
Of Olympos I have come down
To tell you the will of Zeus
And prevent this journey.
Hear me. Hear me now.

Remember my story: my twelve labours,
And my reward, this immortality.
For you, too, there are labours to perform;
For you, too, the rewards are glory and fame.

You will go back with this man to the towers of Troy;
You will find doctors there, to heal your wound;
You will be chosen champion of all the Greeks –
And with this bow, my gift, you will kill

Paris of Troy, who caused this suffering.
You will plunder his city, and carry home
Rich tribute, the prize of the battlefield:
Home to Poias your father and your native land.

Son of Achilles, my words are for your ears too.
Without his help, you will never topple Troy;
Without your help, he too must fall. For you
Are like lions, a pair of lions, joined in the hunt.

I will send doctors to Troy to heal his wound.
The city is doomed to fall, twice, to this bow.
And when you plunder Troy remember this,
This above all: true reverence for the gods.
For nothing is greater in the sight of Zeus
Than reverence. It lives in all men's hearts.
They are mortal, they die; but reverence never dies.

PHILOCTETES

O voice of god; dear friend
I longed to see again –
I hear, I will obey.

NEOPTOLEMOS

I, too, hear and obey.

HERACLES

Lose no more time.
The hour and tide of fate
Are with you. The moment is now.

He disappears.

PHILOCTETES

It is time to say a last farewell
To the cave that watched with me;
The spirits of brooks and fields
And the deep, full-throated roar
Where waves boom on the high cliffs;
My cave-shelter, wet with spray
Borne on the driving wind;
The Hill of Hermes, echoing
My tears, my wintry grief.
It is time to leave the pools,
The bubbling streams; time to take
The unlooked-for gift of fate.

O Lemnos, my island, smile on me,
Send me safe sailing; I go
Where great Destiny leads, my friends'
Advice, and the all-powerful god
Who chose what has happened here.

SAILORS

Gather now, and pray
To the spirits of the sea
To lead us safely home.

Notes

1 The passage about the nightingale is a reference to the story of two sisters, Philomela and Procne. Procne's husband, King Tereus, raped his sister-in-law Philomela, and to prevent her telling anyone, cut out her tongue. But Philomela embroidered what had happened on a piece of needlework, and sent it to her sister Procne. In revenge for what her husband had done, Procne murdered their son Itys, and fed his flesh to his father for dinner. Tereus drew his sword to kill the sisters, but the gods intervened. They changed Tereus into a hoopoe, Philomela into a swallow and Procne into a nightingale. Ever afterwards, the call of the nightingale (in Greek poetry *Itun*, *Itun*) has represented the sobbing of Procne as she weeps for her dead son.

Niobe was a royal princess. She had seven sons and seven daughters, and boasted that she had done better than the goddess Leto, who only had one of each. But Leto's children were the god and goddess of hunting (Apollo and Artemis), and they punished Niobe by shooting her children dead. Niobe was changed into a column of stone (or in some versions a mountainside), still weeping human tears to this day.

2 The Furies were avenging spirits from the underworld, who hunted down and punished criminals (especially criminals who had harmed their own relatives). They are likened sometimes to hunting-dogs, sometimes to winged, evil creatures with women's voices and faces. In some versions of the Agamemnon story (not this play) Orestes is pursued by them for murdering his mother.

3 Pelops, Agamemnon's grandfather, as a young man asked to marry Hippodameia, the daughter of the King of Elis. He was promised her hand, if he could beat her father in a chariot-race. Pelops bribed Myrtilus, the king's charioteer, to take out the linch-pin of the royal chariot. So he won the race, and Hippodameia. But instead of paying Myrtilus as he promised, he hurled him into the sea. As Myrtilus drowned, he cursed Pelops and all his descendants – the beginning of the line of disaster for all the royal house of Argos.

4 An important feature of many surviving Greek plays is a long, descriptive speech from a messenger or other servant, reporting a disaster crucial to the plot. It is possible that these 'messenger's speeches' were a recognised feature of the stage-production too, and followed a regular pattern familiar to the audience. The idea of the messenger's speech as a kind of 'turn' in the theatre is given an ironic twist in this play: the servant's narration of the chariot-race is *precisely* a 'turn', a made-up story whose effect has been exactly calculated in advance. The over-literariness of some of the lines, and the wealth of supporting detail (a characteristic feature of the long-planned lie) are missed by Clytemnestra, Electra and the Chorus; but the 'staginess' of this speech was surely meant to be apparent to the theatre audience. Dramatic irony of this kind (where the audience know more than the characters) is a consistent feature of Sophocles' style.

5 Amphiaraus was a legendary king of one of the smaller cities in Argos. When Oedipus' son Polynices began gathering an army to attack Thebes (see *Antigone*), he bribed Amphiaraus' wife, by giving her a gold necklace, to persuade her husband to join the expedition. Both of them knew that the gods had prophesied that no hero would return from Thebes alive. Amphiaraus was persuaded, went and died. After death he became one of the lesser rulers of the underworld, and a prophetic shrine was built to him near Oropos, which was still in use in Roman times.

6 The story of Niobe is told in note 1. Sipylos was the name of the mountainside.

7 The three myths referred to in this chorus all concern people of royal blood who were cruelly imprisoned. The moral is drawn that what is fated will happen, and there is no way for mortals to prevent it.

Danaë's father was told by an oracle that she would bear a son who was destined to kill him. To prevent her ever becoming pregnant, he imprisoned her in a bronze tower. But Zeus himself came to her, appearing in a shower of golden raindrops. She conceived, and bore a son (Perseus) who, when he grew up, fulfilled the oracle.

Lycurgus was a king who opposed the power of the god Dionysos (like Pentheus in Euripides' *Bacchae*). In punishment, the god sent him mad. His behaviour became so violent and strange that his people, the Edonians, imprisoned him in a cave.

Cleopatra (not the famous queen of Egypt) was the wife of Phineus, King of Salmydessos near the Bosporos. Her husband fell in love with another woman, and banished Cleopatra to a cave. His new wife blinded Cleopatra's children with the sharp shuttle of a loom. This blindness (like the blindness of men to fate) is as important to Sophocles' meaning here as the imprisoning of Cleopatra.

8 In the original Greek production (which used, apart from the Chorus, only three actors) this part, and that of Heracles at the end, were played by the same actor as played Odysseus. We may wonder if the audience was aware of this doubling (as we are when, for example, Claudius and the Ghost are doubled in *Hamlet*), and if so, what effect it had on the meaning and interpretation of the parts concerned.

Further reading

Of the dozens of important books on Sophocles, only a handful are mentioned here, as directly relevant to the style or interpretation adopted in this translation. The principal edition used throughout was that of Jebb (Cambridge University Press, 1890, 1894, 1900), and I had at my elbow the spare, dramatic translations of Watling (Penguin Books, 1947, 1953). Useful works of criticism were Kitto's *Greek Tragedy* (Methuen, 1939) and *Form and Meaning in Drama* (Methuen, 1956), and above all Waldock's *Sophocles the Dramatist* (Cambridge University Press, 1951) and Knox's *The Heroic Temper* (University of California Press, 1966).